ENGLISH
FOR EVERYONE

PHRASAL VERBS

AUDIO GRATUITO
web y app
www.dkefe.com

Autores

Thomas Booth ha trabajado durante 10 años como profesor de inglés en Polonia, Rumanía y Rusia. Actualmente vive en Inglaterra, donde trabaja como editor y autor de materiales para el aprendizaje del inglés. Ha participado en varios libros de la serie *English for Everyone*.

Ben Ffrancon Davies es un escritor y traductor independiente. Escribe libros y guías para el estudio de temas como la enseñanza del inglés, la música y la literatura. Ben estudió lenguas medievales y modernas en la Universidad de Oxford y ha enseñado inglés en Francia y en España.

Asesor de inglés británico

Peter Dainty estudió Historia en la Universidad de Oxford y ha enseñado inglés como lengua extranjera desde hace 40 años. Ha sido profesor de la Universidad de Londres durante 10 años y ha escrito 14 libros para editoriales como Macmillan, Penguin, Scholastic y Oxford University Press.

Asesora de inglés estadounidense

La profesora emérita **Susan Barduhn** ha participado en numerosas publicaciones. Ha sido presidenta de la IATEFL, directora de The Language Center, de Nairobi, subdirectora de International House, de Londres, y profesora y directora del programa MATESOL del SIT Graduate Institute. Actualmente es asesora educativa independiente del Departamento de Estado de Estados Unidos, del British Council, de TransformELT, de The Consultants-e y de Fulbright.

ENGLISH
FOR EVERYONE

PHRASAL VERBS

DK

DK LONDRES
Edición sénior Ben Ffrancon Davies
Edición de arte sénior Clare Shedden, Amy Child
Ilustración Gus Scott
Edición ejecutiva Christine Stroyan
Edición de arte ejecutiva Anna Hall
Edición de producción George Nimmo
Control de producción Samantha Cross
Diseño de cubierta Surabhi Wadhwa-Gandhi
Desarrollo del diseño de cubierta Sophia MTT
Dirección editorial Andrew Macintyre
Dirección de arte Karen Self
Dirección de publicaciones Jonathan Metcalf

DK NUEVA DELHI
Edición sénior Janashree Singha
Edición Nandini D. Tripathy, Rishi Bryan
Edición de arte sénior Vikas Sachdeva
Edición del proyecto de arte Sourabh Challariya
Diseño de maqueta sénior Tarun Sharma
Maquetación Manish Upreti, Anita Yadav
Diseño de cubierta sénior Suhita Dharamjit
Edición ejecutiva de arte sénior Arunesh Talapatra
Edición ejecutiva Soma B. Chowdhury
Dirección de preproducción Balwant Singh, Sunil Sharma
Jefatura editorial Glenda Fernandes
Jefatura de diseño Malavika Talukder

EDICIÓN EN ESPAÑOL
Coordinación editorial Cristina Gómez de las Cortinas
Asistencia editorial y producción Malwina Zagawa

Servicios editoriales Tinta Simpàtica
Traducción Ruben Giró Anglada

Publicado originalmente en Gran Bretaña en 2021 por
Dorling Kindersley Limited
DK, One Embassy Gardens, 8 Viaduct Gardens, London, SW11 7BW
Parte de Penguin Random House

Copyright © 2021 Dorling Kindersley Limited
© Traducción española: 2021 Dorling Kindersley Limited

Título original: *English For Everyone: English Phrasal Verbs*
Primera edición: 2021

ISBN: 978-0-7440-4859-9

Impreso y encuadernado en China

Para mentes curiosas

www.dkespañol.com

MIXTO
Papel procedente de
fuentes responsables
FSC™ C018179

Este libro se ha impreso con papel
certificado por el Forest Stewardship
Council ™ como parte del compromiso
de DK por un futuro sostenible.
Para más información, visita
www.dk.com/our-green-pledge

Contenidos

Cómo utilizar este libro

English for Everyone: phrasal verbs está pensado para aprender, entender y recordar los phrasal verbs más habituales del inglés. Cada una de las 56 unidades del libro contiene una parte teórica sobre un tema, con frases ilustradas para situar los verbos en su contexto, y una parte práctica con ejercicios para reforzar lo que has aprendido. Escucha el audio y repite cada phrasal verb y frase. Encontrarás las respuestas a todos los ejercicios al final del libro, junto con un completo índice.

Número de unidad El libro está dividido en unidades. El número de unidad te ayuda a seguir tu progreso.

Frases de ejemplo Una frase de ejemplo sitúa cada phrasal verb en su contexto (ver página 8).

Número de módulo Cada módulo tiene su número para que te sea fácil localizar el audio correspondiente.

15 Tiempo

Inglés británico o inglés estadounidense Se indica qué phrasal verbs son propios del inglés del Reino Unido (UK) o de Estados Unidos (US).

Formas base y definiciones Debajo de cada frase aparece el verbo en su forma principal y su definición.

Espacio para escribir Es útil que escribas aquí tu propia traducción de los phrasal verbs: así crearás unas útiles páginas de referencia personalizadas.

Módulos Muchas partes teóricas se dividen en módulos con diferentes aspectos del mismo tema.

15.1 TIEMPO

The journey dragged on for hours. The kids were so bored!
drag on
continuar mucho tiempo (negativo)

Time's getting on now. Let's hurry home before it gets dark.
get on (UK)
hacerse tarde (la hora)

We take the children to the park every afternoon to break up the day.
break up
dividir (un día o un período de tiempo) en partes diferentes

The doctor's busy at the moment, but I'll try to fit you in later today.
fit in
hacer tiempo para algo

Mikhail dragged out his speech for so long that some of the audience fell asleep.
drag out
hacer que algo dure demasiado (negativo)

As the years went by, I grew to love Phil's sense of humor.
go by
pasar (el tiempo)

The deadline for the project crept up on us.
creep up (on)
pasarle algo lentamente a alguien sin darse cuenta

I enjoy whiling away the hours reading novels and comic books.
while away
pasar el tiempo de un modo relajado

Danny wasn't able because he ran ou
run out (of)
quedarse sin (tiempo)

Cleaning the hous Liam's weekend.
take up
ocupar, gastar (el tiem

Your session has t Please log in again
time out
cerrarse la sesión en un servidor o sitio web por

Commuting to an eats into my time.
eat into
hacer perder demasiad

15.2 ESPERA

Hi Sally! Can you hang on a minute while I grab my umbrella?
hang on
esperar poco tiempo (informal)

The service here is terrible! It's holding everyone up.
hold up
hacer retrasarse a algo o alguien

Chris was sitting ir his girlfriend to ar
wait for
quedarse en algún sitio algo hasta que pase alg

72

Ejercicio de escucha Este símbolo indica que debes escuchar el audio antes de responder a las preguntas del ejercicio.

Número de ejercicio Los números de los ejercicios te ayudarán a localizar las respuestas.

Respuesta de ejemplo La primera respuesta ya está escrita, para que entiendas mejor el ejercicio.

Instrucciones En cada ejercicio tienes unas breves instrucciones que te indican qué debes hacer.

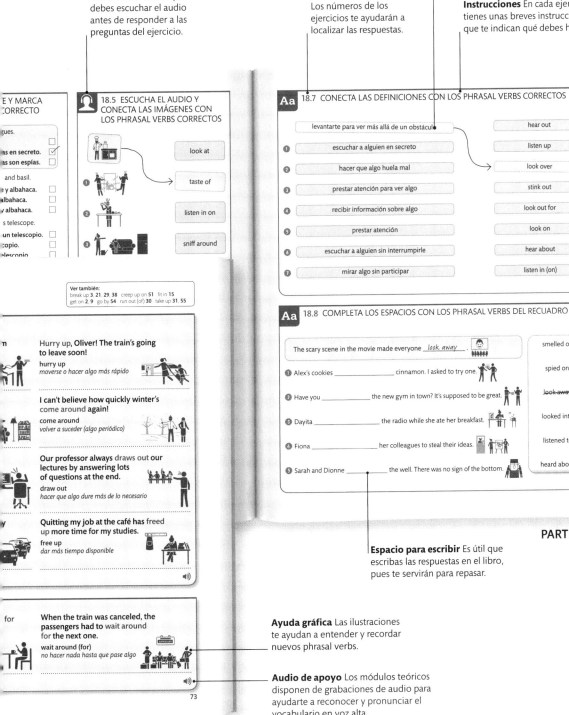

E Y MARCA CORRECTO

...gues.

...as en secreto. ☐
...as son espías. ☑

...and basil.
...y albahaca. ☐
...albahaca. ☐
...y albahaca. ☐

...s telescope.
...un telescopio. ☐
...copio. ☐
...elescopio ☐

18.5 ESCUCHA EL AUDIO Y CONECTA LAS IMÁGENES CON LOS PHRASAL VERBS CORRECTOS

look at

taste of

listen in on

sniff around

Ver también:
break up 3, 21, 38 creep up on 51 fit in 15
get on 2, 9 go by 54 run out (of) 30 take up 31, 55

Aa **18.7** CONECTA LAS DEFINICIONES CON LOS PHRASAL VERBS CORRECTOS

levantarte para ver más allá de un obstáculo

① escuchar a alguien en secreto

② hacer que algo huela mal

③ prestar atención para ver algo

④ recibir información sobre algo

⑤ prestar atención

⑥ escuchar a alguien sin interrumpirle

⑦ mirar algo sin participar

hear out

listen up

look over

stink out

look out for

look on

hear about

listen in (on)

Aa **18.8** COMPLETA LOS ESPACIOS CON LOS PHRASAL VERBS DEL RECUADRO

The scary scene in the movie made everyone _look away_ .

① Alex's cookies _____ cinnamon. I asked to try one.

② Have you _____ the new gym in town? It's supposed to be great.

③ Dayita _____ the radio while she ate her breakfast.

④ Fiona _____ her colleagues to steal their ideas.

⑤ Sarah and Dionne _____ the well. There was no sign of the bottom.

smelled of

spied on

~~look away~~

looked into

listened to

heard about

87

Espacio para escribir Es útil que escribas las respuestas en el libro, pues te servirán para repasar.

PARTE PRÁCTICA

Hurry up, Oliver! The train's going to leave soon!
hurry up
moverse o hacer algo más rápido

I can't believe how quickly winter's come around again!
come around
volver a suceder (algo periódico)

Our professor always draws out our lectures by answering lots of questions at the end.
draw out
hacer que algo dure más de lo necesario

Quitting my job at the café has freed up more time for my studies.
free up
dar más tiempo disponible

When the train was canceled, the passengers had to wait around for the next one.
wait around (for)
no hacer nada hasta que pase algo

73

Ayuda gráfica Las ilustraciones te ayudan a entender y recordar nuevos phrasal verbs.

Audio de apoyo Los módulos teóricos disponen de grabaciones de audio para ayudarte a reconocer y pronunciar el vocabulario en voz alta.

7

Frases de ejemplo

Todos los phrasal verbs están acompañados por una frase de ejemplo que contextualiza su significado. También se ofrece su forma principal y definición.

Phrasal verb El phrasal verb aparece destacado en cada frase.

Ilustración Cada frase incluye una ilustración para mostrar el significado del phrasal verb.

Angela meets up with her colleagues once a week to discuss all their new ideas.

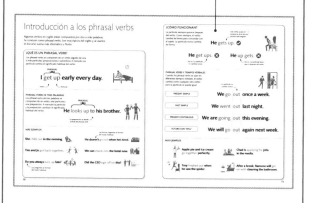

Forma principal
El phrasal verb aparece en su forma principal.

meet up (with)
get together with

Definición
La definición te permitirá entender mejor el significado.

Tercera partícula La tercera partícula de un phrasal verb aparece escrita entre paréntesis cuando es opcional (ver página 12).

Ver también

Muchos phrasal verbs tienen más de un significado. Cada unidad tiene un recuadro "Ver también" que indica otras unidades en las que aparecen los mismos phrasal verbs, pero con significados distintos.

Número de unidad Indica en qué otra unidad aparece el phrasal verb.

Ver también:
push back **16**

AR EL CONFLICTO

leagues always make fun s, but he just laughs it off.

las críticas o a
difícil riéndote

Introducción

Las páginas 10-17 contienen una sección de gramática que explica qué son los phrasal verbs y cómo funcionan a nivel gramatical. También detalla los diferentes tipos de phrasal verbs, así como los sustantivos frasales y los adjetivos frasales.

Aprendizaje por módulos
El apartado de gramática se divide en módulos.

Audio

English for Everyone: phrasal verbs ofrece un gran número de audios de apoyo. Cada phrasal verb y frase de la parte teórica tiene su grabación y es útil que escuches el audio y repitas las expresiones y frases en voz alta hasta que estés seguro de que entiendes y puedes repetir lo que se ha dicho.

AUDIO DE APOYO
Este símbolo indica que están disponibles grabaciones de audio de los phrasal verbs y las frases del módulo para escucharlas.

EJERCICIOS DE ESCUCHA
Este símbolo indica que debes escuchar el audio para poder responder a las preguntas del ejercicio.

AUDIO GRATUITO
web y app
www.dkefe.com

Sección de referencia

Al final del libro, las páginas 230-237 contienen una sección de referencia, que incluye información adicional sobre phrasal verbs, así como ejemplos de sustantivos frasales y adjetivos frasales habituales.

Diagramas visuales
Sirven para presentar las partículas habituales.

Tablas de referencia
Contienen listas de phrasal verbs, sustantivos frasales y adjetivos frasales habituales.

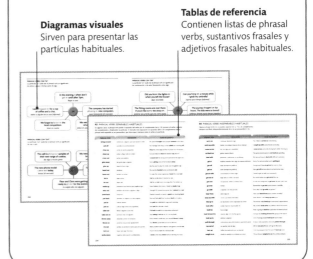

Respuestas

El libro está pensado para que te sea fácil comprobar tu progreso. Incluye las respuestas de todos los ejercicios, con lo que podrás ver si has entendido y recordado los phrasal verbs aprendidos.

Respuestas Tienes las respuestas de todos los ejercicios al final del libro.

Números de ejercicio
Coinciden con el número de la parte superior izquierda de cada ejercicio.

25

25.3
1 The number of peo online shot up last yea
2 The coach divided two equal teams.
3 Shreya counted up wanting coffee and we
4 When Georgia was she added on a 20% tip

25.4
Ⓐ 3 Ⓑ 1 Ⓒ 6 Ⓓ 2

25.5
1 Katie's bills have be a lot of debt now.
2 The company's sha but it's finally starting t
3 The temperature va but it **averages out** at
4 We estimated the to be £14,900, but **rou** nearest thousand

Índice

El índice contiene todos los phrasal verbs de las partes teóricas, además de los sustantivos frasales y adjetivos frasales de la sección de referencia, en orden alfabético, seguidos por el número de unidad y módulo donde aparecen.

Número de módulo
En el índice se indica el mismo número de módulo que en la página de teoría.

Múltiples unidades
Se indican todos los números de módulo de los phrasal verbs que aparecen más de una vez.

Introducción a los phrasal verbs

Algunos verbos en inglés están compuestos por dos o más palabras.
Se conocen como phrasal verbs. Son muy típicos del inglés y, al usarlos,
el discurso suena más idiomático y fluido.

¿QUÉ ES UN PHRASAL VERB?

Los phrasal verbs se componen de un verbo seguido de una
o más partículas (preposiciones o adverbios). A menudo esa
partícula cambia el significado habitual del verbo.

PHRASAL VERB

I get up early every day.

Verbo   Partícula

PHRASAL VERBS DE TRES PALABRAS

Los phrasal verbs de tres palabras se
componen de un verbo, una partícula y
una preposición. A menudo la partícula
y la preposición cambian el significado
habitual del verbo.

PHRASAL VERB

He looks up to his brother.

La preposición se añade
al final del phrasal verb.

MÁS EJEMPLOS

Las formas negativas se forman
del modo habitual.

She chills out in the evening.

He doesn't go out when he's tired.

Tim and Jo got back together.

We can check into the hotel now.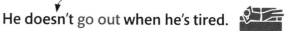

Do you always turn up late?

Las preguntas se forman
del modo habitual.

Did the CEO sign off on this?

¿CÓMO FUNCIONAN?

La partícula siempre aparece después del verbo. Como siempre, el verbo cambia de forma para concordar con el sujeto. La partícula nunca cambia de forma.

Este verbo acaba en "-s" porque es de la tercera persona del singular.

He gets up. ✔

He get ups. ✘

Así no. La partícula no cambia nunca.

He up gets. ✘

Así no. La partícula tiene que ir después del verbo.

PHRASAL VERBS Y TIEMPOS VERBALES

Cuando los phrasal verbs se usan en diferentes tiempos verbales, el verbo cambia como cualquier otro verbo, pero la partícula se queda igual.

La partícula no cambia nunca.

PRESENT SIMPLE	We go **out** once a week.
PAST SIMPLE	We went **out** last night.
PRESENT CONTINUOUS	We are going **out** this evening.
FUTURO CON "WILL"	We will go **out** again next week.

MÁS EJEMPLOS

 Apple pie and ice cream go together **perfectly**.

 Chad is applying for **jobs** in the media.

 Troy freaked out **when** he saw the spider.

 After a break, Ramone will get on with **cleaning the bathroom**.

PHRASAL VERBS TRANSITIVOS E INTRANSITIVOS

Algunos phrasal verbs llevan un complemento directo, el sustantivo que recibe la acción del verbo. Estos se conocen como **verbos transitivos**.

SUJETO	PHRASAL VERB	COMPLEMENTO DIRECTO
Juan	measured out	the ingredients.

Algunos phrasal verbs no llevan un complemento directo. Se conocen como **verbos intransitivos**.

SUJETO	PHRASAL VERB
Tom	woke up.

"Tidy up" se puede usar con o sin complemento directo.

Algunos phrasal verbs pueden ser **transitivos** o **intransitivos**.

SUJETO	PHRASAL VERB	COMPLEMENTO DIRECTO
Idris	tidied up	the mess.

HACER TRANSITIVO UN PHRASAL VERB INTRANSITIVO

Algunos phrasal verbs intransitivos precisan de una preposición para convertirse en transitivos.

At the end of their stay, Julia and John checked out.

At the end of their stay, Julia and John checked out of their hotel.

Añade "of" para usar "check out" con un complemento directo.

MÁS EJEMPLOS

Julian usually heads off early to avoid the traffic.

Julian usually heads off to work early to avoid the traffic.

Ben and Gus finally made up after their argument.

Ben made up with Gus after their argument.

DIFERENTES SIGNIFICADOS

Muchos phrasal verbs tienen más de un significado. Algunos phrasal verbs
aparecen más de una vez en este libro, cada vez con un significado diferente.

SIGNIFICADOS NO RELACIONADOS

El phrasal verb "do up" tiene
dos significados diferentes
por completo.

Mirek did up his coat to keep out the icy breeze.
abrocharse una prenda

Emily is doing up her house at the moment.
mejorar, renovar

....

SIGNIFICADOS LITERALES Y METAFÓRICOS

Algunos phrasal verbs tienen un significado básico
literal y otro metafórico más complicado.

Esta frase utiliza el significado
literal de "break up". Se separa
el chocolate en partes más
pequeñas.

**Patrick broke up the chocolate before
adding it to the cake mixture.**
separar algo en partes más pequeñas

En esta frase no hay nada que
se rompa literalmente, sino
que se nos dice que María
y Pablo se han separado.

**After a huge argument, Maria and
Pablo decided to break up.**
poner fin a una relación afectiva

....

REGISTRO

A pesar de que algunos phrasal verbs se pueden usar en situaciones
formales, la mayoría de ellos son más informales. Muchos phrasal
verbs tienen un equivalente más formal de una sola palabra.

Esta frase usa "persevere", una palabra
de registro elevado que normalmente
solo se usa en registros formales.

**Despite the storm, the engineers persevered
and installed the new phone line.**

Esta frase significa exactamente lo
mismo, pero "soldier on" hace que
la frase sea menos formal.

**Despite the storm, the engineers soldiered on
and installed the new phone line.**

PHRASAL VERBS SEPARABLES

Si un phrasal verb lleva complemento, este a veces puede ir entre el verbo y la partícula, pero esto no cambia su significado. Los phrasal verbs que pueden hacerlo se conocen como phrasal verbs "separables". Consulta la página 234 para ver más ejemplos.

El complemento directo puede ir detrás de la partícula.

He is picking up litter.

He is picking litter up.

El complemento directo también puede ir entre el verbo y la partícula.

He is picking it up.

Si el complemento directo de un phrasal verb separable es un pronombre, tiene que ir entre el verbo y la partícula.

MÁS EJEMPLOS

I turned on **the light.**   I turned **the light** on.

Can you pick up **that box?**   **Can you** pick **that box** up?

You should throw away **those old shoes.**   **You should** throw **those old shoes** away.

I was annoyed because he woke up **the baby.**   **I was annoyed because he** woke **her** up.

I always fill up **the water jug when it's empty.**   **I always** fill **it** up **when it's empty.**

⚠ **ERRORES TÍPICOS** PHRASAL VERBS SEPARABLES

Si el complemento directo de un phrasal verb separable es un pronombre, tiene que ir entre el verbo y la partícula.

Pronombre

El pronombre no puede ir al final de la frase.

He picked it up. ✔   He picked up it.

PHRASAL VERBS INSEPARABLES

Algunos phrasal verbs no se pueden separar. El complemento directo siempre debe ir tras la partícula, nunca puede quedar entre el verbo y la partícula. Esta norma siempre se aplica, al margen de que el complemento directo sea un sustantivo o un pronombre. Consulta la página 235 para ver más ejemplos.

We had to run to get on the train. ✅

El verbo y la partícula
tienen que ir seguidos.

We had to run to get on it. ✅

El verbo y la partícula van seguidos aunque
el complemento directo sea un pronombre.

We had to run to get the train on. ❌

Así no. El complemento directo
no va entre el verbo y la partícula.

MÁS EJEMPLOS

I've come across a new recipe.

I need to go over my notes.

Susan really takes after her father, they're very similar.

He sleeps in most Saturdays.

I ran into her at the supermarket.

Drop by the house any time you like.

PHRASAL VERBS SEPARABLES E INSEPARABLES

Algunos phrasal verbs, como "get back from", pueden ser tanto separables o inseparables, según el contexto.

Si "get back from" significa "recuperar de", es separable. El complemento directo tiene que ir entre "get" y "back".

I finally got my lawnmower back from Dave.

Si "get back from" significa "volver de", siempre es inseparable.

I got back from Italy yesterday.

SUSTANTIVOS FRASALES

Algunos sustantivos se forman a partir de phrasal verbs, a menudo uniendo el verbo y la partícula.

La página 236 contiene una lista con los sustantivos frasales más habituales.

Verbo   Partícula

The teacher asked me to hand out the exam papers.

The teacher gave us a handout for the lesson.

Sustantivo frasal

A veces el sustantivo se forma colocando la partícula delante del verbo.

Oh no! It was sunny and now it's pouring down.

We have a rainy season with daily downpours.

MÁS EJEMPLOS

The company is trying to cut back on staff expenses.

Not another cutback! The company must be in serious trouble.

It's a shame that he wants to drop out of school.

We've had a surprisingly high percentage of dropouts in the class.

We want to get away and go somewhere sunny this winter.

A trip to Australia sounds like a fabulous getaway.

ADJETIVOS FRASALES

Algunos adjetivos se forman a partir de
phrasal verbs, a menudo uniendo el verbo
y la partícula, a veces con un guion.

La página 237
contiene una lista
con los adjetivos
frasales más
habituales.

Verbo   Partícula

Zane asked James to tone down his language.

Zane asked James to use more toned-down language.

Adjetivo frasal

A veces el adjetivo se forma colocando
la partícula delante del verbo.

Anetta is always speaking out about environmental issues.

Anetta is very outspoken about environmental issues.

MÁS EJEMPLOS

**For this yoga position, you
have to stretch your arms out.**

**Simon got into position with
his arms outstretched.**

**Ed watered down his opinion
when writing his review.**

**Ed wrote a watered-down version
of his real opinion for the review.**

**Kemal knocked down the price
of jewelry by 15%.**

**Kemal sold some of his jewelry
at a knockdown price.**

01 Personas y cosas

1.1 PERSONAS

Hundreds of people packed into the town hall to watch the debate.

pack into
llenar un sitio una multitud

I found it really hard to fit in with the art class. They're all much younger than me.

fit in (with)
sentirse parte de un grupo

Some of the older children have been ganging up on me and calling me names.

gang up (on)
formar un grupo contra alguien

Sheila's neighbors look down on her because her house is smaller than theirs.

look down on
creer que eres mejor que otro

I got my son a puppy for his birthday. After asking me for months, he finally wore me down!

wear down
convencer a alguien para que haga lo que quieres (a menudo insistiendo)

I bumped into Sandra at the park. She was asking after you.

ask after
preguntar por alguien

Thousands of fans flooded into the stadium to watch the singer perform.

flood in(to)
entrar una multitud en un lugar

After the concert, everyone spilled out of the stadium and made their way to the train station.

spill out (of)
salir una multitud de un lugar

Ver también:
come across **39**, **52**   fit in **15**   get back (from) **35**
turn to **27**   turn up **4**, **27**

My sister watched over our son while Ania and I went shopping.

watch over
asegurarse de que no le pasa nada malo a alguien o a algo

Adi has got a temper. He turned on me the instant I suggested he buy a new suit.

turn on
atacar a alguien sin previo aviso

Toshiro's been buttering his brother up because he wants to borrow his car.

butter up
alabar o adular a alguien para conseguir algún favor

Jordan's aunts always fuss over him when they come to visit.

fuss over
prestar mucha atención a alguien

Barney really looks up to his grandfather. He loves listening to his stories.

look up to
admirar a alguien

1.2 COSAS

Nuwa gathered up the plates from the table and took them to the kitchen.

gather up
recoger

It was really hard to part with my old car. I'd had it since I was a student.

part with
deshacerse de algo importante para ti

While looking through things in my attic, I came across an old portrait of my great-grandfather.

come across
dar con algo por casualidad

Mel lent Dave her lawnmower a month ago, and she finally got it back from him.

get back (from)
recuperar algo

Ava lost her passport ages ago. It turned up when she was cleaning the living room.

turn up
hallar (generalmente por casualidad)

Aa 1.3 LEE LA FRASE Y MARCA EL SIGNIFICADO CORRECTO

Barney really looks up to his grandfather.
Él quiere a su abuelo. ☐
Él admira a su abuelo. ☑
Él odia a su abuelo. ☐

① After the concert, everyone spilled out of the stadium.
La gente entró simultáneamente al estadio. ☐
Toda la gente dio vueltas al estadio. ☐
La gente salió en masa del estadio. ☐

② Toshiro's been buttering his brother up.
Le ha adulado para obtener un favor. ☐
Le ha estado chillando. ☐
Ha estado discutiendo con él. ☐

③ Sheila's arrogant neighbors look down on her.
Creen que ellos son mejores que ella. ☐
Creen que ella es mejor que ellos. ☐
Creen que ella es maravillosa. ☐

④ I came across an old portrait of my great-grandfather.
Tiré el retrato. ☐
Encontré el retrato por casualidad. ☐
Busqué el retrato. ☐

Aa 1.4 CONECTA CADA IMAGEN CON LA FRASE CORRECTA

I found it hard to fit in with the art class.

① It was hard to part with my old car.

② Sandra was asking after you at the park.

③ Jordan's aunts fuss over him when they visit.

④ Nuwa gathered up the plates from the table.

Aa 1.5 TACHA LAS PALABRAS INCORRECTAS DE CADA FRASE

Hundreds of people packed **into** / ~~over~~ / ~~through~~ the town hall to watch the debate.

① Some of the older children have been **mobbing** / **ganging** / **teaming** up on me and calling me names.

② Ava lost her passport ages ago. It turned **out** / **on** / **up** when she was cleaning the living room.

③ Adi has got a temper. He **pivoted** / **turned** / **rotated** on me the instant I suggested he buy a new suit.

④ Mel lent Dave her lawnmower a month ago, and she finally got it **back** / **forward** / **down** from him.

Aa 1.6 ESCRIBE EL PHRASAL VERB CORRECTO AL LADO DE SU DEFINICIÓN

| recuperar algo | = | *get back (from)* |

① hallar (generalmente por casualidad) = _____

② asegurarse de que no pasa nada malo = _____

③ atacar a alguien sin previo aviso = _____

④ convencer a alguien para que haga algo = _____

⑤ llenar un sitio una multitud = _____

watch over   turn up   wear down   pack into   ~~get back (from)~~   turn on

---

1.7 ESCUCHA EL AUDIO Y COMPLETA LAS FRASES BAJO LAS IMÁGENES

Thousands of fans _____*flooded into*_____ the stadium.

③ I got my son a puppy. After asking me for months, he finally _____ me _____ !

① Some of the older children have been _____ on me and calling me names.

④ Hundreds of people _____ the town hall to watch the debate.

② Mel lent Dave her lawnmower a month ago, and she finally _____ it _____ from him.

⑤ Barney really _____ his grandfather. He loves listening to his stories.

21

02 Familia

2.1 FAMILIA

Dan and Sheila have brought up their children to be kind to animals.

bring up
enseñar a los niños a comportarse

Liam gets on very well with his elder sister. They're always laughing together.

get on (with)
mantener una buena relación con alguien

Colin lives with his son in a house at the edge of town.

live with
compartir la misma casa

Sam wants to be a pilot when he grows up.

grow up
pasar de niño a adulto

Jenny's grown out of her old toys. She prefers playing video games now.

grow out of
perder interés en algo al hacerse mayor

Albert's parents named him after his great-grandfather.

name after
poner el mismo nombre que el de otra persona

2.2 MASCOTAS

Lisa puts her rabbit in its cage each evening before bed.

put in
poner dentro

Fiona's cat doesn't like strangers, but he's warming to Dan.

warm to
encariñarse
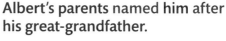

I let the cat out every morning after I've woken up.

let out
dejar salir
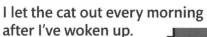

I let the cat in when it started to rain.

let in
dejar entrar

Ver también:
get on **9**, **15**   grow out of **6**   let out **6**
live with **47**   settle down **45**

After traveling for a few years, Bill settled down and bought a house next door to his parents.

settle down
vivir en un sitio

My family pulled together when my father was unwell.

pull together
trabajar juntos para superar una situación complicada

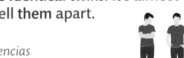

My mother looks after my children while I'm at work.

look after
cuidar, hacerse responsable de

Will and Joe are identical twins. It's almost impossible to tell them apart.

tell apart
reconocer las diferencias

Jasmine takes after her mother. They're very similar people.

take after
tener los rasgos de un progenitor o pariente

Whenever his children stay out late, Carlo waits up until they get home.

wait up
esperar despierto a que alguien llegue a casa

Olly's dog ran away last week while they were at the park.

run away
escaparse

After a few days, Olly's dog came back all by herself.

come back
volver

Aa 2.3 CONECTA CADA IMAGEN CON LA FRASE CORRECTA

① **②** **③**

Olly's dog ran away last week while they were at the park.

My family pulled together when my father was unwell.

My mother looks after my children while I'm at work.

I let the cat in when it started to rain.

Aa 2.4 MARCA LAS FRASES CORRECTAS

My mother looks after my children while I'm at work. ☑
My mother looks over my children while I'm at work. ☐

① After a few days, Olly's dog came back all by herself. ☐
After a few days, Olly's dog came under all by herself. ☐

② Jasmine takes over her mother. They're very similar people. ☐
Jasmine takes after her mother. They're very similar people. ☐

③ I let the cat around every morning after I've woken up. ☐
I let the cat out every morning after I've woken up. ☐

④ Albert's parents named him after his great-grandfather. ☐
Albert's parents named him behind his great-grandfather. ☐

⑤ After traveling for a few years, Bill settled up and bought a house. ☐
After traveling for a few years, Bill settled down and bought a house. ☐

⑥ Colin lives on his son in a house at the edge of town. ☐
Colin lives with his son in a house at the edge of town. ☐

Olly's dog ran _____*away*_____ last week while they were at the park.

1. Lisa puts her rabbit _____ its cage each evening before bed.

2. Will and Joe are identical twins. It's almost impossible to tell them _____ .

3. After traveling for a few years, Bill settled _____ and bought a house next door to his parents.

4. Liam gets _____ very well with his elder sister. They're always laughing together.

5. Fiona's cat doesn't like strangers, but he's warming _____ Dan.

6. Jenny's grown _____ of her old toys, she prefers playing video games now.

| to | down | ~~away~~ | on | apart | out | in |

Sam wants to be a pilot when he _____*grows up*_____ .

1. Will and Joe are identical twins. It's almost impossible to _____ them _____ .

2. Lisa _____ her rabbit _____ its cage each evening before bed.

3. Jasmine _____ her mother. They're very similar people.

4. I _____ the cat _____ every morning after I've woken up.

5. Jenny's _____ her old toys, she prefers playing video games now.

3.1 AMISTADES

Our shared interest in music has really brought us together.

bring together
crear una relación estrecha

I've really gone off Paul since I saw him at the party. He behaved very badly.

go off
gustar menos algo o alguien

Ken stuck by Cath when her restaurant went bankrupt.

stick by
continuar apoyando a alguien en una situación complicada

Misha stood by Colin when he decided to quit college.

stand by
apoyar o defender a alguien cuando los demás no lo hacen

3.2 RELACIONES AFECTIVAS

Jack and Ula really care for each other. They've been together for 50 years.

care for
amar a alguien o quererle mucho

Sonia is trying to win Claude back because she's still in love with him.

win back
persuadir a alguien para recuperar una relación afectiva

I think Pierre has fallen for Clara. Have you seen how he looks at her?

fall for
empezar a amar a alguien, enamorarse

My brother set me up with a woman who works at his office.

set up
prepararle una cita a alguien

Luisa has finished with Ben. He's very upset.

finish with (UK)
acabar una relación con alguien

They started going out with each other when they were at school.

go out (with)
mantener una relación afectiva con alguien

Ver también:
break up **15**, **21**, **29**, **38**   care for **32**   fall for **41**   go off **8**, **27**, **30**, **35**
go out **5**, **27**, **54**   set up **12**, **53**   take out **14**, **21**, **28**

After we left school, my friends and I drifted apart. I became more interested in my career than music.

drift apart
enfriarse lentamente una amistad

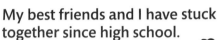

Although I haven't seen Zaira for many years, I always hear from her on my birthday.

hear from
saber algo de

My best friends and I have stuck together since high school.

stick together
permanecer juntos y ayudarse

Bernadette confided in Martha that she was in love with Pavel.

confide in
compartir un secreto con alguien en quien confías

Katia and I dated for a few weeks, but our relationship fizzled out.

fizzle out
perder energía con el paso del tiempo, acabarse lentamente

Robin asked Helen out yesterday. They're going to the movies together.

ask out
invitar a alguien a una cita

For our first date, Phil took me out to an expensive restaurant.

take out
llevar a alguien a una cita

After a huge argument, Maria and Pablo decided to break up.

break up (with)
poner fin a una relación afectiva

Carlos and Mia separated a few months ago, but they recently got back together.

get back together
volver a empezar una relación afectiva

3.3 ESCUCHA EL AUDIO Y LUEGO NUMERA LAS FRASES EN EL ORDEN EN QUE APARECEN

A Robin asked Helen out yesterday. They're going to the movies together. ☐

B I think Pierre has fallen for Clara. Have you seen how he looks at her? ☐

C Our shared interest in music has really brought us together. ☑ 1

D Carlos and Mia separated a few months ago, but they recently got back together. ☐

E After a huge argument, Maria and Pablo decided to break up. ☐

F Although I haven't seen Zaira for many years, I always hear from her on my birthday. ☐

Aa 3.4 COMPLETA LOS ESPACIOS PONIENDO LAS PALABRAS EN SU ORDEN CORRECTO

| up | to | break |

After a huge argument, Maria and Pablo decided __to__ __break__ __up__ .

| me | up | set |

1 My brother _____ _____ _____ with a woman who works at his office.

| for | care | really |

2 Jack and Ula _____ _____ _____ each other. They've been together for 50 years.

| with | going | out |

3 They started _____ _____ _____ each other when they were at school.

| by | stood | Colin |

4 Misha _____ _____ _____ when he decided to quit college.

Aa 3.5 CONECTA LAS DEFINICIONES CON LOS PHRASAL VERBS CORRECTOS

empezar a amar a alguien, enamorarse	fizzle out
❶ gustar menos algo o alguien	drift apart
❷ crear una relación estrecha	fall for
❸ acabarse lentamente	finish with
❹ prepararle una cita a alguien	bring together
❺ enfriarse lentamente una amistad	care for
❻ acabar una relación con alguien	go off
❼ amar a alguien o quererle mucho	set up

Aa 3.6 MIRA LAS IMÁGENES Y COMPLETA LAS FRASES CON PHRASAL VERBS

Katia and I dated for a few weeks, but our relationship ____*fizzled out*____ .

❶ My best friends and I have _____ since high school.

❷ For our first date, Phil _____ me _____ to an expensive restaurant.

❸ Bernadette _____ Martha that she was in love with Pavel.

❹ Luisa has _____ Ben. He's very upset.

❺ Ken _____ Cath when her restaurant went bankrupt.

04 De visita

4.1 DE VISITA

I popped in to see Brian on Saturday morning.

pop in (UK)
visitar a alguien en su casa (informal)

Angelo turned up at my house at 6am. I was still in bed!

turn up
llegar (a menudo de manera inesperada)

On our way home from the beach, we called in to see Grandma.

call in (UK)
visitar a alguien en su casa (a menudo porque queda de paso)

My new neighbors, Kaito and Leiko, had me over for dinner last night.

have over
recibir invitados en casa

It looks like Kia has invited everyone she knows along to the party.

invite along (to)
pedirle a alguien que te acompañe a algún sitio

We chatted for hours, and he suggested I stick around for dinner.

stick around
quedarse en algún sitio más de lo esperado

After chatting on the doorstep for a moment, Malik invited me in.

invite in(to)
pedirle a alguien que entre en tu casa

Following the interview, the secretary showed Connor out.

show out
acompañar a alguien hasta la puerta cuando se va

They showed me around their beautiful home.

show around
enseñar la casa por dentro

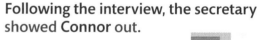

Ver también:
call in **22**, **50** come in **56**
turn up **1**, **27**

4.2 INVITACIÓN A UNA FIESTA

Dear Mason and Emily,

We'd like to invite you over for a barbecue to celebrate Beth's birthday on Saturday. Feel free to come over any time after 2pm, and please bring the kids along, too!

Love, Omar and Beth
P.S. You are all welcome to stay over if you like!

While you're in town, try to swing by. It would be good to see you.

swing by
visitar la casa de alguien de camino hacia otro sitio

....

My father came into the house and took off his coat.

come in(to)
entrar en algún sitio

....

Yesterday afternoon, Liam dropped in for a cup of coffee and a chat.

drop in
visitar a alguien en su casa (informal)

....

On her way home from the gym, Miriam stopped off at the supermarket to get something for dinner.

stop off
realizar una parada en un viaje para hacer algo

....

While everyone was in the garden, I found Klaus snooping around the kitchen.

snoop around
buscar algo en secreto

....

🔊

We'd like to invite you over for a barbecue to celebrate Beth's birthday.

invite over
invitar a alguien a tu casa

....

Omar told us to come over any time after 2pm.

come over
visitar a alguien (en su casa)

....

Mason and Emily brought the kids along to the barbecue.

bring along
llevar a alguien o algo contigo

....

We ended up staying over at Beth and Omar's house.

stay over
pasar la noche en casa de alguien

....

🔊

4.3 ESCUCHA EL AUDIO Y MARCA LOS PHRASAL VERBS QUE APARECEN

come into ☑
pop in ☐

① show around ☐
have over ☐

② invite along ☐
turn up ☐

③ show out ☐
stop off ☐

④ snoop around ☐
swing by ☐

⑤ drop in ☐
stay over ☐

Aa 4.4 LEE LA FRASE Y MARCA EL SIGNIFICADO CORRECTO

I popped in to see Brian on Saturday morning.

Llamé a Brian. ☐
Visité a Brian en su casa. ☑
Invité a Brian a mi casa. ☐

③ Mason and Emily brought the kids along.

Se llevaron a los niños. ☐
Dejaron a los niños. ☐
Llevaron a los niños con ellos. ☐

① Angelo turned up at my house at 6am.

Ha llegado a las 6. ☐
Se ha ido a las 6. ☐
Se ha quedado dormido a las 6. ☐

④ We'd like to invite you over for a barbecue.

Nos gustaría que vinieras a casa. ☐
Nos gustaría que nos llamaras. ☐
Nos gustaría que organizaras una barbacoa. ☐

② They showed me around their beautiful home.

Me pidieron que me fuera. ☐
Me pidieron que pasara. ☐
Me enseñaron su casa. ☐

⑤ Liam dropped in for a cup of coffee and a chat.

Se echó el café encima. ☐
Pasó por casa a visitarme. ☐
Fuimos a tomar café juntos. ☐

Aa 4.5 CONECTA LOS PRINCIPIOS DE LAS FRASES CON LOS FINALES CORRECTOS

Following the interview,	and took off his coat.
1 On her way home from the gym,	I found Klaus snooping around inside.
2 My father came into the house	the secretary showed Connor out.
3 Omar told us to come over	at Beth and Omar's house.
4 After chatting on the doorstep,	Miriam stopped off at the supermarket.
5 We ended up staying over	Malik invited me in.
6 While everyone was in the garden,	any time after 2pm.

Aa 4.6 VUELVE A ESCRIBIR LAS FRASES CORRIGIENDO LOS ERRORES

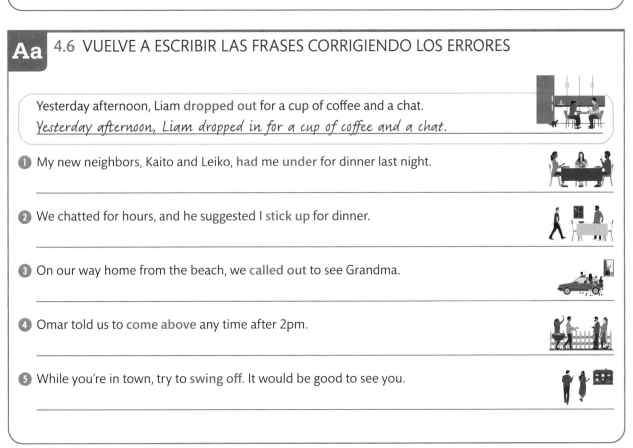

Yesterday afternoon, Liam **dropped out** for a cup of coffee and a chat.
Yesterday afternoon, Liam dropped in for a cup of coffee and a chat.

1 My new neighbors, Kaito and Leiko, **had** me **under** for dinner last night.

_____

2 We chatted for hours, and he suggested I **stick up** for dinner.

_____

3 On our way home from the beach, we **called out** to see Grandma.

_____

4 Omar told us to **come above** any time after 2pm.

_____

5 While you're in town, try to **swing off**. It would be good to see you.

_____

5.1 VIDA SOCIAL

Katie asked Lisa if she wanted to come out to play.

come out
ir a algún lugar con alguien

Once a year, my school friends and I go out for a meal together to catch up.

catch up (with)
hablar con amigos con los que no has hablado últimamente

Chris spends most weekends hanging out with his friends.

hang out (with)
pasar tiempo en un lugar con tus amigos (informal)

As I was leaving for the art exhibition, I asked Joe if he wanted to come along.

come along (with)
acompañar a alguien, ir a algún sitio con alguien

Vincent and Maya decided to stay in. They ordered some pizza and watched a movie.

stay in
quedarse en casa

The carnival was amazing. We stayed out until dawn.

stay out
volver tarde a casa

5.2 IRSE

Joe suddenly took off without saying where he was going.

take off
irse (de manera inesperada)

The movie was terrible, so we slipped out halfway through.

slip out
irse sin avisar

We headed off to the beach early because we wanted to avoid the crowds.

head off (to)
irse, empezar un viaje

Neil was turned away from the nightclub because he was wearing casual clothes.

turn away (from)
no dejar entrar a alguien

Ver también: come along **31**, **52**   come out **12**, **41**   get together **53**
go out **3**, **27**, **54**   hang out **28**   head off (to) **8**   slip out **51**
take off **6**, **9**, **22**, **55**   turn away **19**

Lots of guests were milling around, waiting for Raj to make his speech.

mill around
moverse lentamente por una sala o lugar (a menudo esperando algo)

Amara let her little sister tag along when she went to the ice rink with her friends.

tag along
ir a algún sitio con alguien (a menudo sin invitación)

Fleur and Clare were getting ready to go out for the evening.

go out
ir a algún sitio con alguien, socializar con amigos

Our local hotel has a large room that it hires out for parties.

hire out (UK)
dejar que alguien use algo a cambio de dinero

I was glad to see Marvin at the party. He always manages to liven things up.

liven up
hacer algo más emocionante

Ella likes to get together with her friends at the ice cream parlor on Friday evenings.

get together
encontrarse y estar con amigos

🔊

Charlie stormed out of the store when the manager refused to give him a refund.

storm out (of)
irse de algún sitio porque estás enfadado

I hate to tear you away, but we're going to miss the last train.

tear away (from)
hacer que alguien se vaya de algún sitio a pesar de que se quiera quedar

Paul had to shoot off at the end of the meeting to catch his train home.

shoot off (UK)
irse rápido (informal)

Nadiya had to dash off to pick up the kids from school.

dash off (UK)
irse rápido (informal)

🔊

Aa 5.3 TACHA LAS PALABRAS INCORRECTAS DE CADA FRASE

 Chris spends most weekends hanging ~~up on~~ / out with / ~~in on~~ his friends.

 ❶ Amara let her little sister tag along / about / above when she went to the ice rink.

 ❷ Ella likes to get under / together / on with her friends at the ice cream parlor.

 ❸ I hate to tear you out / away / up, but we're going to miss the last train.

 ❹ Katie asked Lisa if she wanted to come about / on / out to play.

 ❺ Joe suddenly took off / up / in without saying where he was going.

Aa 5.4 COMPLETA LOS ESPACIOS CON LAS PALABRAS DEL RECUADRO PARA CREAR PHRASAL VERBS

Neil was [turned *away from*] the nightclub because he was wearing casual clothes.

❶ Charlie [stormed] the store when the manager refused to give him a refund.

❷ As I was leaving for the art exhibition, I asked Joe if he wanted to [come] .

❸ Lots of guests were [milling] waiting for Raj to make his speech.

❹ Vincent and Maya decided to [stay] . They ordered pizza and watched a movie.

❺ We [headed] the beach early because we wanted to avoid the crowds.

❻ Once a year, my school friends and I go out for a meal together to [catch] .

| along | up | ~~away from~~ | out of | around | off to | in |

36

5.5 ESCUCHA EL AUDIO Y CONECTA LAS IMÁGENES CON LOS PHRASAL VERBS CORRECTOS

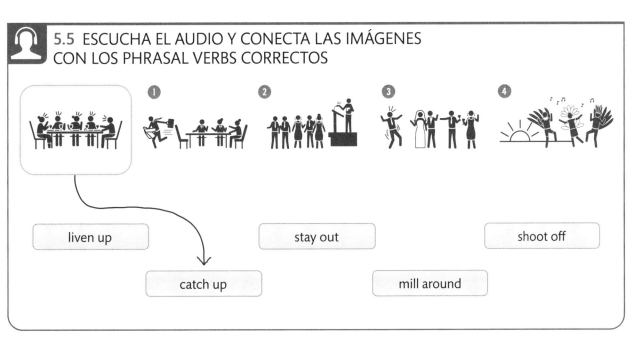

liven up

catch up

stay out

mill around

shoot off

5.6 COMPLETA LOS ESPACIOS PONIENDO LAS PALABRAS EN SU ORDEN CORRECTO

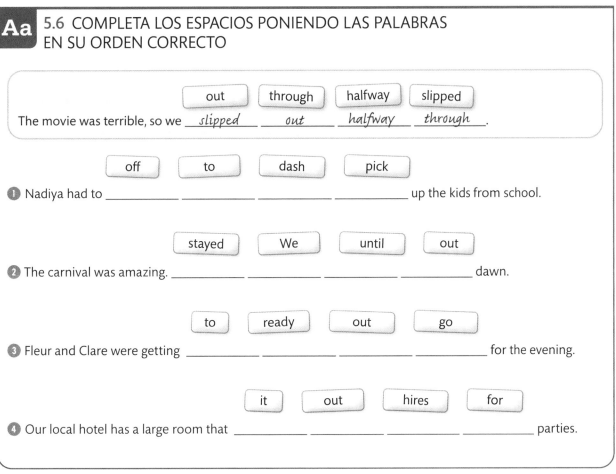

out · through · halfway · slipped

The movie was terrible, so we ___slipped___ ___out___ ___halfway___ ___through___.

off · to · dash · pick

① Nadiya had to _____ _____ _____ _____ up the kids from school.

stayed · We · until · out

② The carnival was amazing. _____ _____ _____ _____ dawn.

to · ready · out · go

③ Fleur and Clare were getting _____ _____ _____ _____ for the evening.

it · out · hires · for

④ Our local hotel has a large room that _____ _____ _____ _____ parties.

6.1 ROPA

Angelica helped her son to button up his shirt as he got ready for school.

button up
abrochar los botones de una prenda

When Tom realized he was late, he threw on a jacket and tie, and ran for the bus.

throw on
ponerse una prenda rápidamente

As Hasan was running across the school yard, one of his shoes came off.

come off
salirse o caerse (una prenda)

All the children at the party had dressed up as dinosaurs.

dress up (as)
ponerse ropa para parecer algo

I hope this juice stain comes out when I wash my shirt.

come out (of)
limpiar, quitar (una mancha)

Gemma's shoes go really well with that dress.

go with
conjuntar con otra prenda

Arnie's so proud of his new jacket. He's been showing it off to everyone.

show off (to)
enseñar a alguien algo de lo que estás orgulloso

Mirek did up his coat to keep out the icy breeze.

do up
abrocharse una prenda

Carly's shoes are too big for her, but she'll grow into them.

grow into
crecer lo suficiente para llevar una prenda

Gio's grown out of his sweater, so he's going to give it to his little brother.

grow out of
crecer demasiado para vestir una prenda

Ver también: come off **26**, **52**   come out (of) **52**   cover up **41**
do up **52**   grow out of **2**   hang up **38**   let out **2**   put on **27**, **41**, **55**
take in **51**, **55**   take off **5**, **9**, **22**, **55**

This dress is a bit too big. We'll need to take it in a little.

take in
arreglar una prenda para hacerla más pequeña

The jacket is too tight. We need to let it out a bit.

let out
arreglar una prenda para hacerla más grande

Kelly stopped to tie up one of her shoe laces.

tie up
abrochar (generalmente los zapatos)

It was very hot in the lecture theater, so Mario took off his sweater.

take off
quitarse (una prenda)

Alex put on her prettiest dress to go out for her wedding anniversary.

put on
llevar puesta una prenda

Make sure you wrap up before heading out into that cold weather.

wrap up
llevar ciertas prendas para mantener el calor

Maurice hung up his coat as he walked in.

hang up
colgar una prenda en una percha o un colgador

Zane folded up his clothes and put them in the wardrobe.

fold up
plegar una prenda

The sun is really strong today, so make sure you cover up.

cover up
protegerse la piel con ropa

Marlon zipped up his leather jacket and walked toward the door.

zip up
cerrar la cremallera de una prenda

6.2 CONECTA CADA IMAGEN CON LA FRASE CORRECTA

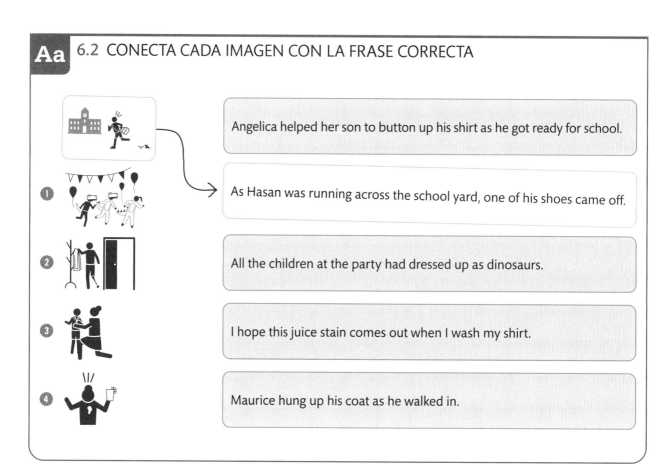

Angelica helped her son to button up his shirt as he got ready for school.

As Hasan was running across the school yard, one of his shoes came off.

All the children at the party had dressed up as dinosaurs.

I hope this juice stain comes out when I wash my shirt.

Maurice hung up his coat as he walked in.

Aa 6.3 MARCA LAS FRASES CORRECTAS

I hope this juice stain comes out when I wash my shirt. ☑
I hope this juice stain comes in when I wash my shirt. ☐

① Marlon zipped up his leather jacket and walked toward the door. ☐
Marlon zipped down his leather jacket and walked toward the door. ☐

② Gemma's shoes go really well about that dress. ☐
Gemma's shoes go really well with that dress. ☐

③ Arnie's so proud of his new jacket. He's been showing it on over everyone. ☐
Arnie's so proud of his new jacket. He's been showing it off to everyone. ☐

④ Zane folded up his clothes and put them in the wardrobe. ☐
Zane folded away his clothes and put them in the wardrobe. ☐

6.4 ESCUCHA EL AUDIO Y NUMERA LAS FRASES EN EL ORDEN EN EL QUE LAS OIGAS

A It was very hot in the lecture theater, so Mario took off his sweater. ☐

B The jacket is too tight. We need to let it out a bit. ☐

C All the children at the party had dressed up as dinosaurs. ☑ 1

D This dress is a bit too big. We'll need to take it in a little. ☐

E Make sure you wrap up before heading out into that cold weather. ☐

F When Tom realized he was late, he threw on a jacket and tie, and ran for the bus. ☐

G Angelica helped her son to button up his shirt as he got ready for school. ☐

Aa 6.5 MIRA LAS IMÁGENES Y COMPLETA LAS FRASES CON PHRASAL VERBS

Carly's shoes are too big for her, but she'll _____*grow into*_____ them.

1 Mirek _____ his coat to keep out the icy breeze.

2 Kelly stopped to _____ one of her shoe laces.

3 The sun is really strong today, so make sure you _____ .

4 Gio's _____ his sweater, so he's going to give it to his little brother.

5 Alex _____ her prettiest dress to go out for her wedding anniversary.

41

7.1 CAUSA Y EFECTO

Heavy traffic has impacted badly on the city's air quality.

impact on
tener un gran efecto sobre algo

Due to her injury, Colleen had to face up to the fact that she couldn't play in the match.

face up to
aceptar y enfrentarse a una mala situación

The heavy rain resulted in floods throughout the city.

result in
hacer que pase algo

The discovery of some ancient ruins has led to an increase in tourism.

lead to
hacer que pase algo

Scientists think that an asteroid colliding with Earth caused the dinosaurs to die out.

die out
desaparecer, extinguirse

The invention of the computer brought about the end of the typewriter.

bring about
hacer que pase algo

🔊

7.2 COMPARACIONES

Old cell phones can't compete with today's smartphones.

compete with
ser algo tan bueno como otra cosa

Sanjay got 100% on his exam. He more than measured up to his parents' expectations.

measure up (to)
cumplir con las expectativas

To get into college, you'll need to improve on last year's results.

improve on
hacer algo mejor que antes

The new action movie really lived up to the crowd's expectations.

live up to
cumplir con las expectativas

🔊

Aa 7.3 CONECTA LAS FRASES QUE SIGNIFICAN LO MISMO

The heavy rain resulted in floods throughout the city.

Old cell phones aren't as good as today's smartphones.

The heavy rain caused floods throughout the city.

1 Heavy traffic has impacted badly on the city's air quality.

2 Old cell phones can't compete with today's smartphones.

Due to her injury, Colleen had to accept the fact that she couldn't play in the match.

3 Due to her injury, Colleen had to face up to the fact that she couldn't play in the match.

To get into college, you'll need to get better results than you got last year.

4 To get into college, you'll need to improve on last year's results.

Heavy traffic has had a strong effect on the city's air quality.

 7.4 ESCUCHA EL AUDIO Y COMPLETA LAS FRASES QUE DESCRIBEN LAS IMÁGENES

 Scientists think that an asteroid colliding with Earth caused the dinosaurs to *die out* .

1  Sanjay got 100% on his exam. He more than _____ his parents' expectations.

2  The new action movie really _____ the crowd's expectations.

3  The discovery of some ancient ruins has _____ an increase in tourism.

4 The invention of the computer _____ the end of the typewriter.

5  The heavy rain _____ floods throughout the city.

8.1 RUTINA DIARIA

My alarm goes off at 7am every morning during the week.

go off
empezar a sonar (un despertador)

Orla went to the bathroom to freshen up before going out.

freshen up
asearse

I usually head off to work at 8 in the morning.

head off (to)
irse, empezar un viaje o un trayecto

Kieran woke up in the middle of the night when he heard a noise outside.

wake up
despertarse

In the evening, I often don't get in until after 7pm.

get in
llegar a casa

Nico usually gets up at about 10am on Saturdays.

get up
salir de la cama

8.4 PHRASAL VERBS SOBRE DORMIR

I tried to wake Mia when I saw she had dozed off at her desk.

doze off
dormirse, a menudo durante el día

On Sunday mornings, I sometimes sleep in as late as 11am.

sleep in
dormir más de lo habitual

Quite a few people nodded off during the speech.

nod off
quedarse dormido (sin querer)

Hanif slept through his alarm again. He's going to be late for work.

sleep through
no despertarse al sonar el despertador

Ver también:
drop off **9**   get in **9**, **53**   get up **53**
go off **3**, **27**, **30**, **35**   head off (to) **5**

8.2 DESCANSO

When Noel got home from work, he sat down and read a book.

sit down
sentarse

Sara was feeling tired, so she lay down on the couch and tried to get some rest.

lie down
tumbarse

Alfred spent the afternoon pottering about in the garden.

potter about
hacer tareas sencillas de forma relajada

8.3 TAREAS

Once the guests had left, Marco set about doing the dishes.

set about (UK)
*empezar a hacer algo
(con energía o entusiasmo)*

After a short break, Ramone got on with cleaning the bathroom.

get on with
*concentrarse en hacer algo
(normalmente tras una pausa)*

Martina stayed up late revising for her exam the following morning.

stay up
quedarse despierto

Uma is still sleeping off the effects of the anesthetic. She'll be able to see you soon.

sleep off
*dormir para recuperarse
(de los efectos de la anestesia)*

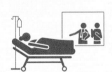

I'm exhausted. I know it's only half past eight, but I'm going to have to turn in.

turn in
irse a la cama

Bradley is sleeping over at his cousin's house tonight. He's so excited about it.

sleep over
*dormir en casa de alguien
(normalmente los niños)*

After a long day at the office, Andrew dropped off in front of the TV.

drop off
quedarse dormido

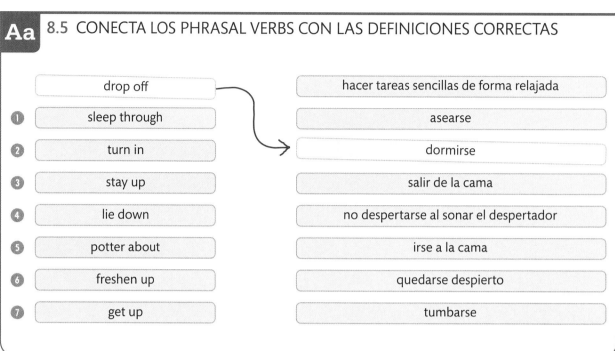

Aa 8.5 CONECTA LOS PHRASAL VERBS CON LAS DEFINICIONES CORRECTAS

drop off	hacer tareas sencillas de forma relajada
1 sleep through	asearse
2 turn in	dormirse
3 stay up	salir de la cama
4 lie down	no despertarse al sonar el despertador
5 potter about	irse a la cama
6 freshen up	quedarse despierto
7 get up	tumbarse

8.6 ESCUCHA EL AUDIO Y MARCA LOS PHRASAL VERBS QUE APARECEN

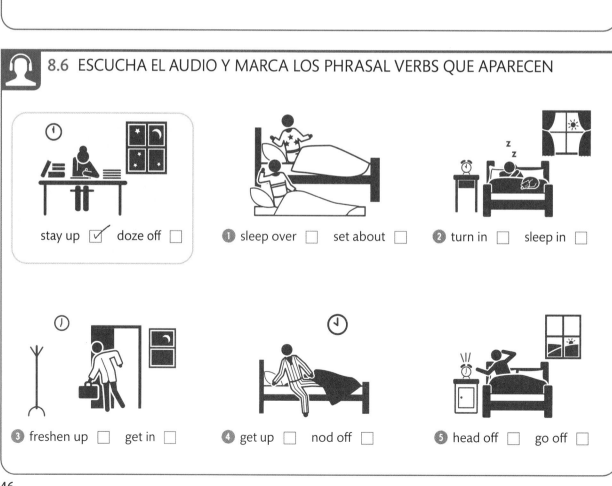

stay up ☑ doze off ☐

1 sleep over ☐ set about ☐

2 turn in ☐ sleep in ☐

3 freshen up ☐ get in ☐

4 get up ☐ nod off ☐

5 head off ☐ go off ☐

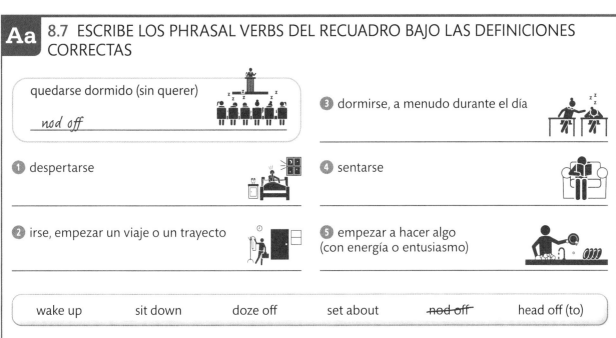

Aa 8.7 ESCRIBE LOS PHRASAL VERBS DEL RECUADRO BAJO LAS DEFINICIONES CORRECTAS

quedarse dormido (sin querer)

nod off

❸ dormirse, a menudo durante el día

_____

❶ despertarse

_____

❹ sentarse

_____

❷ irse, empezar un viaje o un trayecto

_____

❺ empezar a hacer algo (con energía o entusiasmo)

_____

wake up   sit down   doze off   set about   ~~nod off~~   head off (to)

Aa 8.8 COMPLETA LOS ESPACIOS PONIENDO LAS PALABRAS EN SU ORDEN CORRECTO

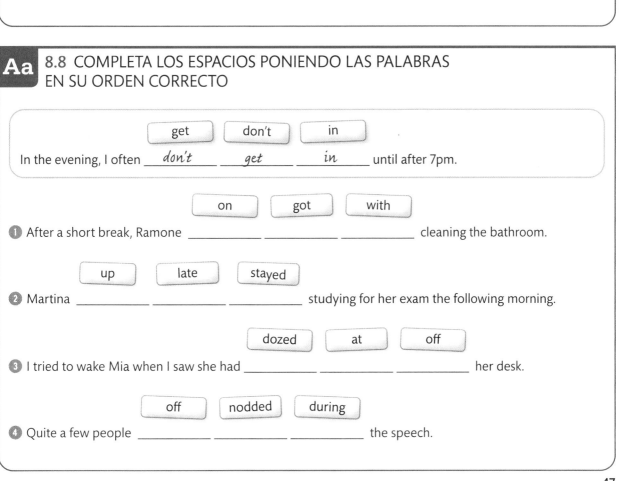

get   don't   in

In the evening, I often ___don't___ ___get___ ___in___ until after 7pm.

on   got   with

❶ After a short break, Ramone _____ _____ _____ cleaning the bathroom.

up   late   stayed

❷ Martina _____ _____ _____ studying for her exam the following morning.

dozed   at   off

❸ I tried to wake Mia when I saw she had _____ _____ _____ her desk.

off   nodded   during

❹ Quite a few people _____ _____ _____ the speech.

09 Transporte

9.1 VEHÍCULOS

Christina's motorcycle broke down while she was traveling through the desert.

break down
dejar de funcionar

Clive tried to restart the motorboat's engine after it cut out without any warning.

cut out
dejar de funcionar de repente

Angelo left his house and got into the taxi.

get in(to)
subir (a un coche o un taxi)

As the movie star got out of the limousine, photographers surrounded him.

get out (of)
bajar (de un coche o un taxi)

George and Yolanda got on the train to Paris.

get on
subir (transporte público)

Gina got off the bus when it arrived at her stop.

get off
bajar (transporte público)

9.2 CONDUCCIÓN

George checked the road for other vehicles before driving off.

drive off
irse

Jen turned back when she realized that she had forgotten her phone.

turn back
volver por donde se acaba de venir

Tanya turned off the main road and drove along the track to the beach.

turn off
dejar una carretera para incorporarse a otra

When you reach the castle, turn onto the highway and head west.

turn onto
tomar una carretera desde otra distinta

Ver también: break down **46**, **50**   cut out **37**   drop off **8**   get in **8**, **53**   get off **22**   get on **2**, **15**   get out **53**, **56**   pick up **10**, **11**, **28**, **31**, **38**   pull over **13**   pull up **28**   take off **5**, **6**, **22**, **55**   turn off **27**

Kamal dropped me off at the train station on his way to work.

drop off
llevar a alguien a algún sitio en coche y dejarle

Sally picked her friends up outside the movie theater at 9pm.

pick up
ir a recoger a alguien (normalmente en coche)

You should always slow down when you drive past a school.

slow down
ir más lento

The train left the station slowly, before speeding up as it headed to the coast.

speed up
ir más rápido

The helicopter took off from the top of the skyscraper.

take off
despegar

The plane touched down in Dubai at 9pm in the evening.

touch down
aterrizar

We pulled in at a small roadside café, where we could have some breakfast.

pull in(to)
detenerse y aparcar

I pulled up by the train station to let my daughter out.

pull up
dejar de circular (por poco tiempo)

Marion didn't notice the motorcycle as she pulled out of the junction.

pull out (of)
pasar de una carretera a otra

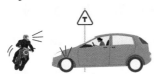

I got lost driving to your house. I had to pull over and ask for directions.

pull over
conducir hacia el arcén de la carretera y detenerse

The helicopter took off from the top of the skyscraper.

❶

George checked the road for other vehicles before driving off.

❷

Gina got off the bus when it arrived at her stop.

❸

I got lost driving to your house. I had to pull over and ask for directions.

❹

The train left the station slowly, before speeding up as it headed to the coast.

❺

Tanya turned off the main road and drove along the track to the beach.

Gina got ~~up~~ / off / ~~through~~ the bus when it arrived at her stop.

❶ Jen turned down / back / up when she realized that she had forgotten her phone.

❷ I pulled up / down / out by the train station to let my daughter out.

❸ Sally picked her friends on / in / up outside the movie theater at 9pm.

❹ When you reach the castle, turn over / onto / with the highway and head west.

❺ Jamie dropped me off / on / in at the train station on his way to work.

❻ Angelo left his house and got into / over / up the taxi.

❼ Marion didn't notice the motorcycle as she pulled over on / out of / up to the junction.

9.5 ESCUCHA EL AUDIO Y COMPLETA LAS FRASES QUE DESCRIBEN LAS IMÁGENES

The train left the station slowly, before _____*speeding up*_____ as it headed to the coast.

③ The plane _____ in Dubai at 9pm in the evening.

❶ As the movie star _____ the limousine, photographers surrounded him.

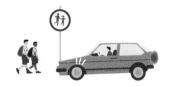

④ You should always _____ when you drive past a school.

❷ We _____ at a small roadside café, where we could have some breakfast.

⑤ Clive tried to restart the motorboat's engine after it _____ without any warning.

Aa 9.6 ESCRIBE EL PHRASAL VERB CORRECTO AL LADO DE SU DEFINICIÓN, COMPLETANDO LAS PALABRAS QUE FALTAN

despegar	=	t a k e o f f
❶ subir (transporte público)	=	g _ _ o _
❷ ir más lento	=	s _ _ _ _ d _ _ _ _
❸ dejar de funcionar	=	b _ _ _ _ _ d _ _ _ _
❹ irse	=	d _ _ _ _ _ o _ _
❺ tomar una carretera desde otra distinta	=	t _ _ _ _ o _ _ _ _

10 De compras

10.1 DE COMPRAS

Once Ellie had found a scarf that she liked, she went to check out.

check out (US)
pagar

Ellie used her credit card to pay for the scarf.

pay for
pagar por algo que estás comprando

Peter bought up all the pizzas in the store before his party.

buy up
comprar todo lo que queda de algo

Aziz had been looking around the store for ages, but couldn't find a shirt he liked.

look around
visitar una tienda y ver qué hay

Joshua crossed off each item on the shopping list as he found it.

cross off
tachar algo de una lista

Luis put the melon in his basket and checked it off his shopping list.

check off (US)
poner una marca junto a algo en una lista

Kemal knocked down the price of jewelry by 15% to attract shoppers to his new store.

knock down
bajar precios

I bought my new laptop online, and went to pick it up at my local store the following day.

pick up
recoger un artículo comprado en línea

My favorite author has just brought out a new novel.

bring out
lanzar a la venta un nuevo producto

Fans are lining up outside the bookstore to buy it.

line up
hacer cola por algo

Ver también:
check out **35**, **50**   pick up **9**, **11**, **28**, **31**, **38**
take back **16**, **44**, **55**

Ethan's going camping this weekend, so he's stocking up on insect repellant.

stock up (on)
comprar mucho de algo por si acaso

The mugs I bought online are broken. I'm going to send them back.

send back
devolver algo por correo al vendedor

Before buying a new car, it's worth shopping around. You might find a bargain.

shop around
visitar varias tiendas (o sitios web) para comparar productos y precios

Aisha decided to splash out on clothes for her summer vacation.

splash out (on)
gastar mucho dinero sin pensárselo demasiado

I went to the market to buy some bread, but they had sold out.

sell out (of)
vender todos los artículos disponibles

Marta couldn't wait to try out her new games console.

try out
probar algo nuevo para ver qué tal

Carla didn't like the sweater she'd bought, so she decided to take it back.

take back
devolver un producto a la tienda donde lo compraste

Shoppers had already snapped up all the bargains at the sale by the time I'd arrived.

snap up
comprar algo en seguida, justo cuando sale al mercado

The fitting rooms are over there if you'd like to try it on.

try on
probarse una prenda para ver cómo queda

 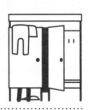

10.2 CONECTA LAS FRASES QUE SIGNIFICAN LO MISMO

My favorite author has just brought out a new novel.

The mugs I bought online are broken. I'm going to return them to the seller by mail.

My favorite author has just put a new novel on sale.

1 The fitting rooms are over there if you'd like to try it on.

2 The mugs I bought online are broken. I'm going to send them back.

I went to the market to buy some bread, but all the bread had been sold.

3 I bought my new laptop online, and went to pick it up at my local store.

The fitting rooms are over there if you'd like to wear the clothes to see if they fit.

4 Before buying a new car, it's worth shopping around to find a bargain.

I bought my new laptop online, and went to collect it from my local store.

5 I went to the market to buy some bread, but they had sold out.

Before buying a new car, it's worth visiting several stores to compare prices.

10.3 ESCRIBE LOS PHRASAL VERBS DEL RECUADRO BAJO LAS DEFINICIONES CORRECTAS

devolver algo por correo al vendedor

send back

3 tachar algo de una lista

1 hacer cola por algo

4 vender todos los artículos disponibles

2 comprar mucho de algo por si acaso

5 comprar algo en seguida, justo cuando sale al mercado

cross off	snap up	line up	sell out (of)	~~send back~~	stock up (on)

10.4 ESCUCHA EL AUDIO Y COMPLETA LAS FRASES QUE DESCRIBEN LAS IMÁGENES

Before buying a new car, it's worth _shopping around_ . You might find a bargain.

1 Marta couldn't wait to _____ her new games console.

2 Kemal _____ the price of jewelry by 15% to attract shoppers to his new store.

3 Luis put the melon in his basket and _____ his shopping list.

4 Aisha decided to _____ clothes for her summer vacation.

5 Ellie used her credit card to _____ the scarf.

10.5 COMPLETA LOS ESPACIOS CON LAS PALABRAS DEL RECUADRO PARA CREAR PHRASAL VERBS

Peter [bought *up*] all the pizzas in the store before his party.

1 Aziz had been [looking] the store for ages, but couldn't find a shirt he liked.

2 Shoppers had already [snapped] all the bargains at the sale by the time I'd arrived.

3 Once Ellie had found a scarf that she liked, she went to [check] .

4 Carla didn't like the sweater she'd bought, so she decided to [take it] .

5 Joshua [crossed] each item on the shopping list as he found it.

| up | back | ~~up~~ | off | out | around |

11 El tiempo

11.1 EL TIEMPO

As dark storm clouds rolled in from the east, Arthur tried to get home before the rain started.

roll in
(el mal tiempo) acercarse

It looks like the weather's clearing up. We'll be able to start the game again soon.

clear up
(el tiempo) destaparse, estar menos nublado

The weather's been awful, but it's finally starting to brighten up.

brighten up
más soleado, menos nublado

Chris and Mel had to leave the beach when it started bucketing down.

bucket down
llover muchísimo (informal)

Once the storm had calmed down, Grace checked her house for damage.

calm down
amainar la tormenta o el viento

Minutes after Ben had lit the grill, the sky clouded over. He hoped it wouldn't rain.

cloud over
nublarse

Don't go outside yet, Pamela. It's pouring down!

Oh, thanks Martin. I'll wait until it eases off a bit.

pour down
llover mucho

ease off
perder fuerza o intensidad

Ver también:
brighten up **45**   calm down **45**   clear up **32**, **50**
cool down **11**   pick up **9**, **10**, **28**, **31**, **38**   warm up **33**

The wind's picking up. It's perfect weather for flying a kite.

pick up
aumentar, cobrar fuerza

As soon as the storm had blown over, the hikers left the cave and continued walking.

blow over
(una tormenta) alejarse

Alice likes to sit on the balcony when the weather cools down in the evening.

cool down
ser más fresco

After days of bad weather, the rain finally started to let up.

let up
perder intensidad

People go ice-skating when the lake freezes over in the winter.

freeze over
congelarse por completo

Ella stood in a bus shelter waiting for the wind to die down.

die down
(una tormenta o el viento) calmarse

Today started off nicely, so we ate our breakfast on the terrace.

start off
empezar

By the end of May, the weather starts to warm up and the tourists start to arrive.

warm up
ser más cálido

Aa 11.2 MARCA LAS FRASES CORRECTAS

Don't go outside yet, Pamela. It's pouring down! ☑
Don't go outside yet, Pamela. It's pouring up! ☐

1. Today started off nicely, so we ate our breakfast on the terrace. ☐
   Today started on nicely, so we ate our breakfast on the terrace. ☐

2. After days of bad weather, the rain finally started to let down. ☐
   After days of bad weather, the rain finally started to let up. ☐

3. Chris and Mel had to leave the beach when it started bucketing under. ☐
   Chris and Mel had to leave the beach when it started bucketing down. ☐

4. The weather's been awful, but it's finally starting to brighten up. ☐
   The weather's been awful, but it's finally starting to brighten off. ☐

Aa 11.3 CONECTA LAS IMÁGENES CON LAS FRASES CORRECTAS

The wind's picking up. It's perfect weather for flying a kite.

1. Ella stood in a bus shelter waiting for the wind to die down.

2. Minutes after Ben had lit the grill, the sky clouded over.

3. People go ice-skating when the lake freezes over in the winter.

4. Alice likes to sit on the balcony when the weather cools down in the evening.

Aa 11.4 VUELVE A ESCRIBIR LAS FRASES CORRIGIENDO LOS ERRORES

> Minutes after Ben had lit the grill, the sky **clouded off**. He hoped it wouldn't rain.
>
> _Minutes after Ben had lit the grill, the sky clouded over. He hoped it wouldn't rain._

1 As soon as the storm had **blown under**, the hikers left the cave and continued walking.

_____

2 As dark storm clouds **rolled out** from the east, Arthur tried to get home before the rain started.

_____

3 It looks like the weather's **clearing off**. We'll be able to start the game again soon.

_____

4 By the end of May, the weather starts to **warm around** and the tourists start to arrive.

_____

5 Once the storm had **calmed up**, Grace checked her house for damage.

_____

🎧 11.5 ESCUCHA EL AUDIO Y LUEGO NUMERA LAS IMÁGENES EN EL ORDEN EN QUE APARECEN

A ☐

B 1

C ☐

D ☐

E ☐

F ☐

G ☐

H ☐

12 Tecnología

12.1 ORDENADORES

To access your account, log in with
your username and password.

log in(to)
entrar en una cuenta o sistema

Always make sure you log out of your
account after using it, so hackers can't
steal your data.

log out (of)
salir de una cuenta o sistema

As soon as Sherelle gets into work,
she boots up her computer.

boot up (UK)
iniciar, encender (un ordenador)

You should shut down your computer
at night to save electricity.

shut down
apagar (un ordenador)

This is the third time that our
system has gone down
this morning!

go down
dejar de funcionar (una red)

I back up all my photos in case my
computer breaks. I keep them
on an external hard drive.

back up
hacer una copia de algo

Some criminals hacked into our computer
system and stole the new designs.

hack into
acceder a un ordenador ilegalmente

Our company hired a technician
to set up the new printer.

set up
dejar algo listo para su uso

12.3 NUEVOS PRODUCTOS

My office has started rolling out some new
software. People are very confused by it.

roll out
(sobre un producto) presentar

The new phone model came out today.
There was a long line outside the store.

come out
(sobre un producto)
salir al mercado

Ver también:
back up **44**   come out **5**, **6**, **12**, **41**, **52**
go down **32**, **54**   set up **3**, **53**

12.2 USO DE LA TECNOLOGÍA

Pete scrolled up to the top of the document to find the company's address.

scroll up (to)
desplazarse hacia arriba (en una página)

I had to scroll down to the bottom of the page to find the information I was looking for.

scroll down (to)
desplazarse hacia abajo (en una página)

When Amy zoomed in, she noticed the red car in front of the restaurant.

zoom in
ver algo más de cerca

Amy zoomed out to look at the whole picture.

zoom out
ver algo más de lejos

You have to type in your password to access the website.

type in
introducir información con un teclado

I type out my essays because it's quicker than writing them by hand.

type out
escribir un texto con un teclado

If you click on the link at the bottom of the page, you will see the answers.

click on
seleccionar algo en una pantalla

I printed out a copy of the contract for the clients to sign.

print out
imprimir algo en papel

The company has started phasing in new computers. They look great!

phase in
(sobre un producto) sacar lentamente al mercado

I agree. I'm so glad that they're phasing these old models out.

phase out
(sobre un producto) sustituir lentamente

12.4 ESCUCHA EL AUDIO Y LUEGO NUMERA LAS FRASES EN EL ORDEN EN QUE APARECEN

A As soon as Sherelle gets into work, she boots up her computer. ☐

B When Amy zoomed in, she noticed the red car in front of the restaurant. 1

C I had to scroll down to the bottom of the page to find the information I was looking for. ☐

D I printed out a copy of the contract for the clients to sign. ☐

E This is the third time that our system has gone down this morning! ☐

F The new phone model came out today. There was a long line outside the store. ☐

G To access your account, log in with your username and password. ☐

Aa 12.5 CONECTA CADA IMAGEN CON LA FRASE CORRECTA

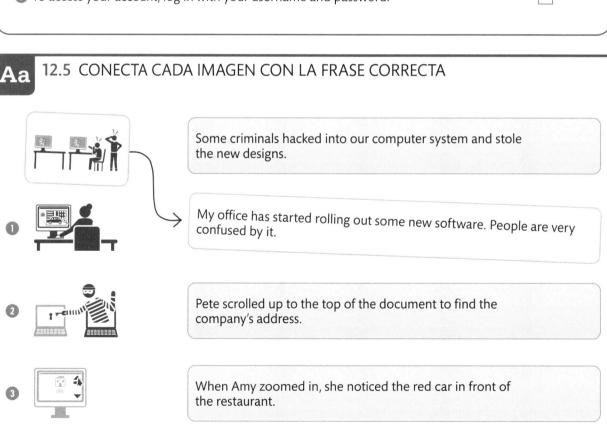

Some criminals hacked into our computer system and stole the new designs.

My office has started rolling out some new software. People are very confused by it.

Pete scrolled up to the top of the document to find the company's address.

When Amy zoomed in, she noticed the red car in front of the restaurant.

Aa 12.6 COMPLETA LOS ESPACIOS CON LOS PHRASAL VERBS DEL RECUADRO

This is the third time that our system has ___*gone down*___ this morning!

1. You should _____ your computer at night to save electricity.

2. _____ the link at the bottom of the page to see the answers.

3. I _____ all my photos in case my computer breaks.

4. Always make sure you _____ of your account after using it.

5. The company has started _____ new computers. They look great!

click on

log out

phasing in

~~gone down~~

shut down

back up

Aa 12.7 VUELVE A ESCRIBIR LAS FRASES CORRIGIENDO LOS ERRORES

To access your account, **log off** with your username and password.
To access your account, log in with your username and password.

1. I **type in** my essays because it's quicker than writing them by hand.
_____

2. I **printed up** a copy of the contract for the clients to sign.
_____

3. Our company hired a technician to **put up** the new printer.
_____

4. You have to **type down** your password to access the website.
_____

5. Amy **zoomed up** to look at the whole picture at once.
_____

13 Delincuencia, justicia y política

13.1 DELINCUENCIA Y JUSTICIA

Gustav broke out of prison by digging a hole under the main wall.

break out (of)
fugarse de una prisión

Someone broke into my house and stole all my jewelry.

break in(to)
entrar en un edificio para robar algo

Phil had to go to the hospital after somebody beat him up.

beat up
causar daños golpeando repetidamente

The police ordered the criminal to hand over the stolen money.

hand over
devolver algo a su propietario

The police are cracking down on illegal parking in the city.

crack down (on)
ser más estricto con la normativa vigente

Janice is leading a campaign to stamp out littering in the park.

stamp out
hacer que algo malo o desagradable deje de suceder

The police cordoned off the area where the crime had taken place.

cordon off
evitar la entrada en una área con una barrera

Dan tipped off the police about the location of the stolen artworks.

tip off
proporcionar información anónima a alguien

After robbing the store, the thieves got away in a stolen car.

get away
escaparse

The police could tell from the tire tracks that the thieves had escaped by car.

tell from
sacar conclusiones de las pruebas

Ver también:
get away **35**   pull over **9**
turn to **21**, **45**, **50**

The local government has brought in a new law banning cars from entering the city center.

bring in
aprobar una nueva ley

Watch out for pickpockets when you're on the train!

watch out for
ser consciente de un peligro

While I was driving home, the traffic police pulled me over for speeding.

pull over
hacer parar a un conductor por haber hecho algo ilegal

The detectives tracked down the thief using fingerprints on the door handle.

track down
trabajar para encontrar a alguien o algo

My brother turned to crime after he lost his job.

turn to
empezar a hacer algo diferente

🔊

13.2 POLÍTICA

Activists are calling on the government to protect the country's forests.

call on
pedir públicamente a alguien que actúe

Senators voted on the new law after a long debate.

vote on
decidir sobre una ley votando

The protestors are calling for better public transportation in the town.

call for
pedir públicamente que pase algo

One of my old school friends is running for mayor.

run for
ser candidato a un cargo político

I'm definitely going to vote for her.

vote for
apoyar a alguien o algo por medio del voto

🔊

Aa 13.3 CONECTA LAS FRASES QUE SIGNIFICAN LO MISMO

Someone broke into my house and stole all my jewelry.

The police stopped people from entering the area where the crime had taken place.

1. One of my old school friends is running for mayor.

Someone entered my house without permission and stole all my jewelry.

2. The police cordoned off the area where the crime had taken place.

The police are becoming stricter on illegal parking in the city.

3. After robbing the store, the thieves got away in a stolen car.

Be aware of pickpockets when you're on the train!

4. Watch out for pickpockets when you're on the train!

Activists are asking the government publicly to protect the country's forests.

5. The police are cracking down on illegal parking in the city.

One of my old school friends is a candidate for mayor.

6. Activists are calling on the government to protect the country's forests.

After robbing the store, the thieves escaped in a stolen car.

13.4 ESCUCHA EL AUDIO Y LUEGO NUMERA LAS IMÁGENES EN EL ORDEN EN QUE APARECEN

 **A** ☐

 **B** 1

 **C** ☐

 **D** ☐

 **E** ☐

 **F** ☐

 **G** ☐

 **H** ☐

13.5 MARCA LAS FRASES CORRECTAS

Gustav broke out of prison by digging a hole under the main wall. ☑
Gustav smashed out of prison by digging a hole under the main wall. ☐

1 The police ordered the criminal to foot over the stolen money. ☐
The police ordered the criminal to hand over the stolen money. ☐

2 Senators voted on the new law after a long debate. ☐
Senators voted about the new law after a long debate. ☐

3 Janice is leading a campaign to stamp out littering in the park. ☐
Janice is leading a campaign to stamp on littering in the park. ☐

4 While I was driving home, the traffic police grabbed me over for speeding. ☐
While I was driving home, the traffic police pulled me over for speeding. ☐

5 Dan tipped off the police about the location of the stolen artworks. ☐
Dan tipped up the police about the location of the stolen artworks. ☐

13.6 ESCRIBE EL PHRASAL VERB CORRECTO AL LADO DE SU DEFINICIÓN

sacar conclusiones de las pruebas	=	*tell from*
1 apoyar a alguien o algo por medio del voto	=	
2 empezar a hacer algo diferente	=	
3 trabajar para encontrar a alguien o algo	=	
4 causar daños golpeando repetidamente	=	
5 aprobar una nueva ley	=	
6 pedir públicamente que pase algo	=	

14.1 DINERO

Dan has owed me £200 for six months, but he's finally paid up.

pay up
devolver (a menudo a regañadientes) todo el dinero que te han dejado

---

I've decided to cut back on spending by bringing my own lunch to work.

cut back (on)
gastar menos dinero

I came into a lot of money when my grandfather died.

come into
recibir de golpe; heredar

Sara has finally coughed up the money I lent her last year.

cough up
pagar deudas (a regañadientes)

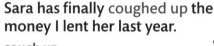

I lent Jenny $20 yesterday and she paid me back today.

pay back
devolver el dinero que te han dejado

Tommy had to fork out more than $600 to get his car repaired.

fork out (for)
gastar mucho dinero en algo

Nura asked Craig's friends to chip in $5 each toward his birthday present.

chip in
aportar dinero entre todos

More than a million dollars was wiped off the price of our company this morning.

wipe off
perder valor

Gary lives off the money that he inherited from his aunt. He does not need to work.

live off
obtener dinero suficiente de algún lugar para poder pagar todo lo necesario

I try to live on half my paycheck every month so I can save the rest.

live on
tener la cantidad de dinero justa para comprar lo básico

Ver también:
add up **25**, **41**   come to **24**   cut back **28**   pay off **26**
run into **26**   take out **3**, **21**, **28**   wipe off **21**

The cost of the new stadium has already run into the millions.

run into
dejar que una deuda ascienda hasta una cifra determinada

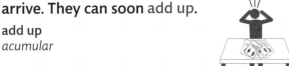

Tara and Ali are saving up for a new house. They try to save $300 each month.

save up
ahorrar dinero (para algo concreto)

Try to pay your bills as soon as they arrive. They can soon add up.

add up
acumular

Patrick went to the bank to pay in some cash.

pay in(to)
meter dinero en el banco

Pete went to the ATM to take out some cash.

take out
sacar dinero del banco

Nick doesn't earn much money, but it's enough to get by.

get by
tener el dinero justo para sobrevivir

The food was excellent, but we were shocked when the bill came to more than $200.

come to
llegar a una cantidad concreta

Wayne paid for everyone's lunches yesterday, so we settled up with him today.

settle up (with)
pagar a alguien lo que le debes

Colin has run up some huge debts renovating his house.

run up
dejar que crezca una deuda o una cuenta

He doesn't know how he's going to pay them off.

pay off
acabar de devolver el dinero que te han dejado

Aa 14.2 LEE LA FRASE Y MARCA EL SIGNIFICADO CORRECTO

I lent Jenny $20 yesterday and she paid me back today.

Jenny tiró 20 dólares. ☐

Jenny me devolvió 20 dólares. ☑

Jenny me robó 20 dólares. ☐

① More than a million dollars was wiped off the price of our company this morning.

La empresa ha perdido valor. ☐

La empresa ha ganado valor. ☐

La empresa ha cerrado. ☐

② Tommy had to fork out more than $600 to get his car repaired.

Tommy gastó mucho dinero. ☐

Tommy ahorró mucho dinero. ☐

Tommy pidió dinero prestado. ☐

③ I came into a lot of money when my grandfather died.

Perdí mucho dinero. ☐

Heredé mucho dinero. ☐

Doné mucho dinero. ☐

④ Patrick went to the bank to pay in some cash.

Patrick sacó dinero del banco. ☐

Patrick ingresó dinero en el banco. ☐

Patrick atracó un banco. ☐

⑤ Wayne paid for everyone's lunches yesterday, so we settled up with him today.

Le quitamos el dinero a Wayne. ☐

Compartimos dinero con Wayne. ☐

Pagamos a Wayne lo que le debíamos. ☐

Aa 14.3 ESCRIBE LOS PHRASAL VERBS DEL RECUADRO DEBAJO DE LAS DEFINICIONES CORRECTAS

tener el dinero justo para sobrevivir

get by

① devolver (a menudo a regañadientes) todo el dinero que te han dejado

_____

② perder valor

_____

③ dejar que crezca una deuda o una cuenta

_____

④ aportar dinero entre todos

_____

⑤ tener la cantidad de dinero justa para comprar lo básico

_____

⑥ ahorrar dinero (para algo concreto)

_____

pay up   ~~get by~~   live on   run up

chip in   save up   wipe off

Aa 14.4 VUELVE A ESCRIBIR LAS FRASES CORRIGIENDO LOS ERRORES

> He doesn't know how he's going to **pay** them **over**.
> *He doesn't know how he's going to pay them off.*

1 Sara has finally **coughed on** the money I lent her last year.

_____

2 I've decided to **cut down for** spending by bringing my own lunch to work.

_____

3 The food was excellent, but we were shocked when the bill **went to** more than $200.

_____

4 The cost of the new stadium has already **run through** the millions.

_____

5 Try to pay your bills as soon as they arrive. They can soon **add on**.

_____

14.5 ESCUCHA EL AUDIO Y ESCRIBE LAS FRASES BAJO LAS IMÁGENES

Gary lives off the money that he inherited.

1 _____

2 _____

3 _____

4 _____

5 _____

15 Tiempo

15.1 TIEMPO

The journey dragged on for hours. The kids were so bored!

drag on
continuar mucho tiempo (negativo)

Mikhail dragged out his speech for so long that some of the audience fell asleep.

drag out
hacer que algo dure demasiado (negativo)

Time's getting on now. Let's hurry home before it gets dark.

get on (UK)
hacerse tarde (la hora)

As the years went by, I grew to love Phil's sense of humor.

go by
pasar (el tiempo)

We take the children to the park every afternoon to break up the day.

break up
dividir (un día o un período de tiempo) en partes diferentes

The deadline for the project crept up on us.

creep up (on)
pasarle algo lentamente a alguien sin darse cuenta

The doctor's busy at the moment, but I'll try to fit you in later today.

fit in
hacer tiempo para algo

I enjoy whiling away the hours reading novels and comic books.

while away
pasar el tiempo de un modo relajado

15.2 ESPERA

Hi Sally! Can you hang on a minute while I grab my umbrella?

hang on
esperar poco tiempo (informal)

The service here is terrible! It's holding everyone up.

hold up
hacer retrasarse a algo o alguien

Ver también:
break up **3**, **21**, **29**, **38**   creep up on **51**   fit in **15**
get on **2**, **9**   go by **54**   run out (of) **30**   take up **31**, **55**

Danny wasn't able to finish the exam because he ran out of time.

run out (of)
quedarse sin (tiempo)

Cleaning the house took up all of Liam's weekend.

take up
ocupar, gastar (el tiempo)

Your session has timed out. Please log in again.

time out
cerrarse la sesión en un ordenador, servidor o sitio web por inactividad

Commuting to and from work really eats into my time.

eat into
hacer perder demasiado (tiempo)

Hurry up, Oliver! The train's going to leave soon!

hurry up
moverse o hacer algo más rápido

I can't believe how quickly winter's come around again!

come around
volver a suceder (algo periódico)

Our professor always draws out our lectures by answering lots of questions at the end.

draw out
hacer que algo dure más de lo necesario

Quitting my job at the café has freed up more time for my studies.

free up
dar más tiempo disponible

Chris was sitting in the café waiting for his girlfriend to arrive.

wait for
quedarse en algún sitio o posponer algo hasta que pase algo

When the train was canceled, the passengers had to wait around for the next one.

wait around (for)
no hacer nada hasta que pase algo

Winter's come around again so quickly!

Se ha acabado el invierno.	☐
El invierno ha vuelto a llegar.	✓
El invierno aún no ha empezado.	☐

❶ Hurry up, Oliver! The train's going to leave soon!

Frena, Oliver.	☐
Deja de caminar, Oliver.	☐
Apresúrate, Oliver.	☐

❷ Quitting my job has freed up time for my studies.

Tengo más tiempo para estudiar.	☐
Tengo menos tiempo para estudiar.	☐
No tengo tiempo para estudiar.	☐

❸ As the years went by, I grew to love Phil.

Empecé a querer a Phil.	☐
No quiero a Phil.	☐
Siempre he querido a Phil.	☐

❹ Our professor always draws out our lectures.

Sus lecciones son cortas.	☐
Sus lecciones son muy largas.	☐
No quiere dar lecciones.	☐

❺ I enjoy whiling away the hours reading.

Leo muy rápido.	☐
Leo muy poco rato.	☐
Me gusta pasar el rato leyendo.	☐

❻ He ran out of time and could not finish the exam.

Le han dado más tiempo.	☐
Se le ha acabado el tiempo.	☐
Todavía le ha quedado algo de tiempo.	☐

❼ Your session has timed out. Please log in again.

Tu sesión ha finalizado por falta de actividad.	☐
Tu sesión continúa abierta.	☐
No has iniciado la sesión.	☐

 15.4 ESCUCHA EL AUDIO Y MARCA LOS PHRASAL VERBS QUE APARECEN

free up ✓   free down ☐

drag out ☐   drag in ☐

❶ drag out ☐   drag in ☐

❷ hurry in ☐   hurry up ☐

❸ wait out ☐   wait for ☐

❹ break up ☐   break in ☐

❺ while over ☐   while away ☐

15.5 COMPLETA LOS ESPACIOS CON LOS PHRASAL VERBS DEL RECUADRO

As the years ___went by___ , I grew to love Phil's sense of humor.

eats into

❶ The journey _____ for hours. The kids were so bored.

crept up on

❷ Commuting to and from work really _____ my time.

~~went by~~

❸ Cleaning the house _____ all of Liam's weekend.

took up

❹ The deadline for the project _____ us.

dragged on

15.6 COMPLETA LOS ESPACIOS PONIENDO LAS PALABRAS EN SU ORDEN CORRECTO

| wait | for | around |

Passengers had to ___wait___ ___around___ ___for___ the next train.

| up | everyone | holding |

❶ The service here is terrible! It's _____ _____ _____ .

| on | now | getting |

❷ Time's _____ _____ _____ . Let's hurry home before it gets dark.

| a | hang | on |

❸ Can you _____ _____ _____ minute while I grab my umbrella?

| fit | in | you |

❹ The doctor's busy today, but I'll try to _____ _____ _____ tomorrow.

16.1 FUTURO

The building project has just begun. Months of construction work lie ahead before it'll be finished.

lie ahead
quedar por delante

Elly and George are looking forward to going to the beach later.

look forward to
esperar algo con muchas ganas

All the streets were decorated in the weeks leading up to the festival.

lead up to
pasar durante el período anterior a un acontecimiento

Colin is working hard because the deadline for his article is coming up.

come up
acercarse, pasar en breve

Kira had dreamed of becoming a great actor, but her plans didn't pan out.

pan out
producirse, hacerse realidad

🔊

16.2 RECUERDOS

Being at the beach stirs up memories of vacations with my grandmother.

stir up
hacer que alguien piense en el pasado

Roland looks back on his college days with pleasure.

look back (on)
recordar, pensar en el pasado

Finding my old toys brought back happy memories of my childhood.

bring back
hacer que alguien piense en el pasado

16.3 CAMBIOS

The house was turned into a convenience store in the 1980s.

turn into
convertirse, transformarse en

We are planning to turn it back into a house and live there.

turn back into
volver a su forma original

Ver también:
bring back **35**   come up **36, 50, 52**   go back **35, 54**
push back **43**   take back **10, 44, 55**

When I recognized Roshan, memories of our days in Delhi came flooding back.

flood back
recuperar recuerdos o emociones de repente

Peter reminds me of you when you were a little boy.

remind of
hacer que alguien recuerde a una persona, lugar o acontecimiento del pasado

I like to listen to music and think back to my days as a musician in Paris.

think back (to)
pensar sobre un acontecimiento del pasado

This dress takes me back to my childhood in the 1960s.

take back (to)
hacer que alguien piense en el pasado

Many of the buildings in my city date back to the 19th century.

date back to
empezar a existir en un momento concreto del pasado

The doctor's off this afternoon, so could we bring your appointment forward to 11 o'clock this morning?

bring forward (to)
avanzar

Claude is unwell today. We'll have to push our meeting back to tomorrow.

push back (to)
atrasar una cita, posponer

In my country, the clocks go forward one hour in the spring.

go forward
adelantar

The clocks go back one hour in the fall.

go back
atrasar

16.4 ESCUCHA EL AUDIO Y LUEGO NUMERA LAS IMÁGENES EN EL ORDEN EN QUE APARECEN

A ☐

B 1

C ☐

D ☐

E ☐

F ☐

G ☐

H ☐

Aa 16.5 TACHA LAS PALABRAS INCORRECTAS DE CADA FRASE

The house was turned ~~out~~ / into / ~~over~~ a convenience store in the 1980s.

1 In my country, the clocks go **forward** / **away** / **under** one hour in the spring.

2 The clocks go **back to** / **again in** / **back** one hour in the fall.

3 Elly and George are looking **on to** / **out of** / **forward to** going to the beach later.

4 Claude is unwell today. We'll have to push our meeting back **away** / **to** / **out** tomorrow.

5 Finding my old toys brought **back** / **over** / **in** happy memories of my childhood.

6 The building project has just begun. Months of construction work lie **ahead** / **under** / **above**.

7 We are planning to turn the store back **around** / **over** / **into** a house and live there.

8 All the streets were decorated in the weeks leading **up** / **down** / **over** to the festival.

Being at the beach stirs up memories

my childhood in the 1960s.

1 This dress takes me back to

when you were a little boy.

2 Kira had dreamed of becoming a

of vacations with my grandmother.

3 Peter reminds me of you

a convenience store in the 1980s.

4 Many of the buildings in my city

great actor, but her plans didn't pan out.

5 The house was turned into

date back to the 19th century.

Many of the buildings in my city **date back on** the 19th century.
Many of the buildings in my city date back to the 19th century.

1 The doctor's off tomorrow, so could we **bring** your appointment **forward on** today?

_____

2 Colin is working hard because the deadline for his article is **coming down**.

_____

3 Roland **looks out on** his college days with pleasure.

_____

4 All the streets were decorated in the weeks **leading over to** the festival.

_____

5 I like to listen to music and **think forward to** my days as a musician in Paris.

_____

6 The building project has just begun. Months of construction work **lie before**.

_____

17.1 HACER PLANES

Kwang had been planning to study medicine, but ended up studying French.

end up
hacer algo diferente a lo que habías planeado al principio

My dad wanted to buy a motorcycle for ages, but I never expected him to go through with it.

go through with
hacer algo que habías planeado hacer (tras haberlo pensado o hablado)

The negotiating teams stayed up until after midnight hammering out a new treaty.

hammer out
llegar a un acuerdo tras una ardua discusión

We want to get married in summer, but we haven't pinned down a location yet.

pin down
decidir sobre los detalles de algo

I asked Sabrina if she wanted to go camping, but she threw out the idea.

throw out
rechazar una recomendación o una idea

Giovanni forgot about the art project, but he managed to throw something together.

throw together
hacer algo sin prepararlo

17.2 CANCELAR PLANES

Ed had promised to do a bungee jump with me, but backed out at the last minute.

back out
no hacer algo que habías acordado hacer

Dexter was going to ask Becky out on a date, but he chickened out.

chicken out
decidir no hacer algo que habías planeado hacer porque te da miedo (informal)

Adi always manages to wriggle out of helping with the cleaning.

wriggle out of
evitar hacer algo que deberías hacer (informal)

Ver también:
end up **35**   get out of **31**
throw out **39**

You should plan ahead before setting off on a long car journey.

plan ahead
hacer planes antes de que pase algo, con antelación

Allow for **traffic delays when estimating how long it'll take.**

allow for
tener algo en cuenta antes de planear algo

You need to think ahead and save some money for the future.

think ahead
pensar en el futuro y planearlo

The two directors had several meetings to firm up the details of the new contract.

firm up
definir más algo

We've been meaning to get a new kitchen for years, but we never get around to it.

get around to
encontrar tiempo para hacer algo

Look ahead and picture what you want to be doing in five years' time.

look ahead
pensar sobre qué podría pasar en el futuro

The store weaseled out of giving us a refund by claiming we had broken the vase.

weasel out of
evitar hacer algo que habías acordado hacer de una manera poco elegante (informal)

Seb said he'd help me paint the house, but he went back on his promise.

go back on
no ser capaz de mantener un acuerdo o una promesa

Cleo didn't want to go out, so she pretended to be sick to get out of it.

get out of
evitar hacer algo que habías acordado hacer

Seb said he'd help me paint the house, but he went back on his promise.

The two directors had several meetings to make the new contract more definite.

① Allow for traffic delays when estimating how long the journey will take.

Seb said he'd help me paint the house, but he did not keep his promise.

② We've been meaning to get a new kitchen for years, but we never get around to it.

I asked Sabrina if she wanted to go camping, but she rejected the idea.

③ Giovanni forgot about the art project, but he managed to throw something together.

We've been meaning to get a new kitchen for years, but haven't found the time for it.

④ The two directors had several meetings to firm up the details of the new contract.

Take traffic delays into consideration when estimating how long the journey will take.

⑤ I asked Sabrina if she wanted to go camping, but she threw out the idea.

The negotiating teams stayed up to discuss and reach an agreement on a new treaty.

⑥ The negotiating teams stayed up until after midnight hammering out a new treaty.

Giovanni forgot about the art project, but he managed to do it without preparation.

We want to get married, but we haven't _pinned down_ a location yet.

hammering out

① They stayed up until after midnight _____ a new treaty.

think ahead

② Cleo pretended to be sick to _____ going out.

pinned down

③ Dexter was going to ask Becky out, but he _____ .

get out of

④ You need to _____ and save money for the future.

chickened out

Kwang had been planning to study medicine, but _____*ended up*_____ studying French.

③ _____ and picture what you want to be doing in five years' time.

① You should _____ before setting off on a long car journey.

④ The store _____ giving us a refund by claiming we had broken the vase.

② Seb said he'd help me paint the house, but he _____ his promise.

⑤ Ed had promised to do a bungee jump with me, but _____ at the last minute.

🎧 17.6 ESCUCHA EL AUDIO Y LUEGO NUMERA LAS FRASES EN EL ORDEN EN QUE APARECEN

🅐 My dad wanted to buy a motorcycle for ages, but I never expected him to go through with it. ☐

🅑 We want to get married in summer, but we haven't pinned down a location yet. ☐

🅒 I asked Sabrina if she wanted to go camping, but she threw out the idea. ☑ 1

🅓 We've been meaning to get a new kitchen for years, but we never get around to it. ☐

🅔 Kwang had been planning to study medicine, but ended up studying French. ☐

🅕 Seb said he'd help me paint the house, but he went back on his promise. ☐

🅖 Giovanni forgot about the art project, but he managed to throw something together. ☐

18 Los sentidos

18.1 OÍDO

Listen up! You're going to fail your exam unless you start working a bit harder.

listen up
prestar atención

Andy hid behind the curtain so he could listen in on Carmen and Simon's conversation.

listen in (on)
escuchar a alguien a escondidas

Dayita listened to the radio while she ate her breakfast.

listen to
prestar atención a alguien que habla o algo que hace algún ruido

Marion asked her son to listen out for the doorbell while she was in the garden.

listen out for
escuchar con atención para oír un ruido concreto

Have you heard about the new gym in town? It's supposed to be great.

hear about
recibir información sobre algo

Please hear me out! I don't want to be a lawyer. I want to be an actor!

hear out
escuchar a alguien sin interrumpirle

18.2 OLFATO Y GUSTO

Alex's cookies smelled of cinnamon. I asked to try one.

smell of
oler a algo

Whatever Pablo has cooked is stinking the whole house out.

stink out
hacer que algo huela mal (informal)

That journalist's been sniffing around again trying to find out what's going on.

sniff around
intentar encontrar información

This soup is delicious! It tastes of tomato and basil.

taste of
saber a algo

Ver también:
look into **20**

18.3 VISTA

Robert has been looking for his glasses all afternoon. He can't find them anywhere.

look for
buscar algo

The geologist looked at each of the rocks. They were unlike anything he'd seen before.

look at
examinar algo

We all looked on in silence as the magician seemed to cut the person in half.

look on
mirar algo sin participar

While you're in the national park, look out for bald eagles near the rivers and lakes.

look out for
prestar atención para ver algo

The children looked over the wall, trying to see where the ball had landed.

look over
levantarte para ver más allá de un obstáculo

The scary scene in the movie made everyone look away.

look away
apartar la mirada de algo

Sarah and Dionne looked into the well. There was no sign of the bottom.

look into
mirar dentro de un agujero, una habitación o un objeto vacío para ver qué hay

Marcus looked through his telescope to see the moon.

look through
mirar a través de algo para ver qué hay en el otro lado

Vineeta's summer house has the perfect location. It looks out over a lake.

look out over
tener vistas hacia

Fiona spied on her colleagues to steal their ideas.

spy on
espiar, mirar a alguien en secreto

Aa 18.4 LEE LA FRASE Y MARCA EL SIGNIFICADO CORRECTO

Fiona spied on her colleagues.

Fiona es una espía. ☐
Fiona miraba a sus colegas en secreto. ☑
Fiona cree que sus colegas son espías. ☐

❶ The soup tastes of tomato and basil.

La sopa solo tiene tomate y albahaca. ☐
La sopa sabe a tomate y albahaca. ☐
A la sopa le falta tomate y albahaca. ☐

❷ Marcus looked through his telescope.

Marcus se ha comprado un telescopio. ☐
Marcus ha visto un telescopio. ☐
Marcus ha utilizado su telescopio. ☐

❸ Robert looked for his glasses.

Robert quería recuperar sus gafas. ☐
Robert buscaba sus gafas. ☐
Robert se compró unas gafas nuevas. ☐

❹ Please hear me out!

¡Escúchame! ☐
¡Sal conmigo! ☐
¡Déjame en paz! ☐

18.5 ESCUCHA EL AUDIO Y CONECTA LAS IMÁGENES CON LOS PHRASAL VERBS CORRECTOS

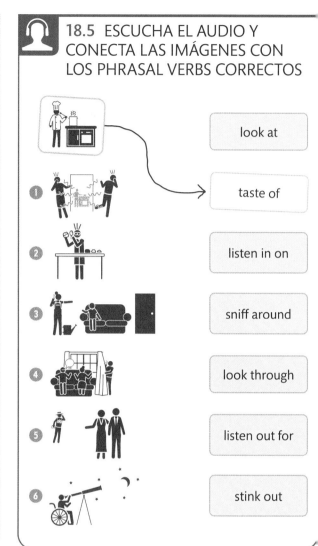

look at

taste of

listen in on

sniff around

look through

listen out for

stink out

Aa 18.6 ESCRIBE EL PHRASAL VERB CORRECTO AL LADO DE SU DEFINICIÓN, COMPLETANDO LAS LETRAS QUE FALTAN

mirar algo sin participar = <u>l o o k</u> <u>o n</u>

❶ intentar encontrar información sobre alguien o algo = <u>s _ _ _ _</u> <u>a _ _ _ _ _</u>

❷ examinar algo = <u>l _ _ _</u> <u>a _</u>

❸ tener vistas hacia = <u>l _ _ _</u> <u>o _ _</u> <u>o _ _ _</u>

❹ apartar la mirada de algo = <u>l _ _ _</u> <u>a _ _ _</u>

Aa 18.7 CONECTA LAS DEFINICIONES CON LOS PHRASAL VERBS CORRECTOS

Definiciones	Phrasal verbs
levantarte para ver más allá de un obstáculo	hear out
1 escuchar a alguien en secreto	listen up
2 hacer que algo huela mal	look over
3 prestar atención para ver algo	stink out
4 recibir información sobre algo	look out for
5 prestar atención	look on
6 escuchar a alguien sin interrumpirle	hear about
7 mirar algo sin participar	listen in (on)

Aa 18.8 COMPLETA LOS ESPACIOS CON LOS PHRASAL VERBS DEL RECUADRO

The scary scene in the movie made everyone _look away_ .

1 Alex's cookies _____ cinnamon. I asked to try one.

2 Have you _____ the new gym in town? It's supposed to be great.

3 Dayita _____ the radio while she ate her breakfast.

4 Fiona _____ her colleagues to steal their ideas.

5 Sarah and Dionne _____ the well. There was no sign of the bottom.

smelled of

spied on

look away

looked into

listened to

heard about

19.1 MOVIMIENTO Y PROGRESO

Martin was exhausted, and began to fall behind the other runners.

fall behind
moverte más lento que la gente de tu alrededor

The rain made it hard for the hikers to keep going, but they pressed on.

press on
continuar pese a las dificultades

Tanya turned away as the nurse gave her the injection.

turn away
girar la cabeza o el cuerpo para dejar de tener algo delante

The security guards told us to stop taking photos of the building and move along.

move along
abandonar un lugar (normalmente dicho por alguien con autoridad)

As the train went through the mountain range, Ted took some photographs.

go through
moverse por una habitación o un espacio

There was a loud knock at the door. Hassan stood up and went to answer it.

stand up
levantarse tras estar sentado

The saleswoman came up to Fabio and asked if he needed any help.

come up to
acercarse a alguien

As we came down from the summit, the weather became much worse.

come down (from)
moverse hacia la base de algo

The monkey climbed up the tree with Kazuo's camera.

climb up
subir a algún sitio (a menudo usando los brazos y las piernas)

Kazuo got the monkey to climb down by offering it a banana.

climb down
bajar de algún sitio (a menudo usando los brazos y las piernas)

Ver también:
climb down **44**   fall behind **20**   get down **46**, **53**
go through **54**   turn around **33**   turn away **5**

Terry doubled back when he realized he'd walked past the entrance to the gallery.

double back
dar media vuelta e irte por donde acabas de venir

When I heard someone calling my name, I turned around.

turn around
girar hasta quedar en dirección contraria

Clive lifted his daughter up so that she could see the deer.

lift up
levantar a alguien o algo

Doug dropped back to help one of the other hikers, who had injured himself.

drop back
empezar a moverse más lento que el resto

Helen told her son to get down from the garden wall.

get down (from)
bajar hacia el suelo o una posición más baja

19.2 PHRASAL VERBS CON "WALK"

The visitors walked around the palace gardens.

walk around
moverte a pie por un sitio

The explorers walked into the cave.

walk in(to)
entrar a pie en una habitación, edificio o espacio cerrado

A line of tourists slowly walked over the ancient bridge.

walk over
pasar a pie por encima de un sitio

While we were chatting, Mani walked off without saying where he was going.

walk off
irse a pie (a menudo sin dar explicaciones)

Janine grabbed her coat and walked out of the room.

walk out (of)
abandonar una habitación, edificio o espacio cerrado a pie

19.3 ESCUCHA EL AUDIO Y LUEGO NUMERA LAS FRASES EN EL ORDEN EN QUE APARECEN

A While we were chatting, Mani walked off without saying where he was going. ☐

B Terry doubled back when he realized he'd walked past the entrance to the gallery. ☐

C There was a loud knock at the door. Hassan stood up and went to answer it. 1

D The rain made it hard for the hikers to keep going, but they pressed on. ☐

E The security guards told us to stop taking photos of the building and move along. ☐

Aa **19.4** CONECTA LOS PRINCIPIOS DE LAS FRASES CON LOS FINALES CORRECTOS

Janine grabbed her coat → and walked out of the room.

① Kazuo got the monkey to climb — down by offering it a banana.

② The explorers walked — into the cave.

③ Doug dropped back to help one of — the other hikers, who had injured himself.

④ As we came down from the summit, — the weather became much worse.

⑤ The saleswoman came up — to Fabio and asked if he needed any help.

⑥ Clive lifted his daughter up — so that she could see the deer.

Aa 19.5 TACHA LAS PALABRAS INCORRECTAS DE CADA FRASE

 A line of tourists slowly walked ~~around~~ / **over** / ~~through~~ the ancient bridge.

 ❶ When I heard someone calling my name, I turned **about** / **around** / **off**.

 ❷ Martin was exhausted, and began to **fall** / **run** / **jump** behind the other runners.

 ❸ Clive lifted his daughter **over** / **down** / **up** so that she could see the deer.

 ❹ Janine grabbed her coat and walked **back** / **out** / **down** of the room.

 ❺ Doug dropped **out** / **in** / **back** to help one of the other hikers, who had injured himself.

Aa 19.6 COMPLETA LOS ESPACIOS PONIENDO LAS PALABRAS EN SU ORDEN CORRECTO

| the | walked | around |

The visitors ___walked___ ___around___ ___the___ palace gardens.

| away | as | turned |

❶ Tanya _____ _____ _____ the nurse gave her the injection.

| climbed | the | up |

❷ The monkey _____ _____ _____ tree with Kazuo's camera.

| get | from | down |

❸ Helen told her son to _____ _____ _____ the garden wall.

| the | through | went |

❹ As the train _____ _____ _____ mountain range, Ted took some photographs.

20 Estudiar e investigar

20.1 ESTUDIAR E INVESTIGAR

I'm moving to Tokyo for a year. I need to **brush up on** my Japanese.

brush up on
practicar, revisar

Nadia stayed up all night trying to **work out** the answer to the equation.

work out
solucionar un problema

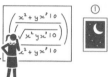

The library was full of students swotting up on English grammar.

swot up on (UK)
(informal) estudiar una asignatura

I kept making mistakes trying to answer the question, so decided to start over.

start over (US)
volver a empezar

Fiona worked through the problems in her code to fix the issues.

work through
enfrentarse a un problema de manera diligente y metódica

Sam has dived into his new project. He spent all weekend working on it.

dive in(to)
empezar a hacer algo con entusiasmo

Patsy's research focuses on space travel.

focus on
prestar atención a

She's looking into how astronauts might travel to Mars one day.

look into
investigar o descubrir sobre algo

20.2 PRESENTACIONES

At the start of your presentation, lay out the main points you are going to discuss.

lay out
presentar o explicar de manera clara

After introducing your topic, you should then move on to presenting each of your arguments.

move on (to)
pasar al punto siguiente

Ver también:
fall behind **20**   keep up with **33**   look into **20**
move on **45**   work out **26**, **33**   work through **45**

Hi, Arjun. Do you know what "burdensome" means?

No, I don't. You'll have to look it up in a dictionary.

look up
encontrar información en línea o en un libro de referencia

The practical assessment and the written exam both **count toward** your final grade.

count toward
contar para

Bill is trying to **cram in** as much studying as possible before the exam.

cram in (UK)
Dedicarse con intensidad durante un corto espacio de tiempo

Emma was sick for most of the spring. She has **fallen behind** the other students in her year.

fall behind
no seguir el ritmo

Even though Leo is the youngest in his class, he manages to **keep up with** the other children.

keep up with
progresar a igual velocidad que alguien

Noah is **majoring in** international politics at college. He hopes to become an ambassador one day.

major in (US)
especializarse en algo en la universidad

Please take care writing your presentation. You'll be **marked down for** incorrect spelling.

mark down
bajarle la nota a alguien

At the end of your presentation, you should **sum up** each of your conclusions.

sum up
hacer un resumen en las conclusiones

Aa 20.3 MARCA LAS FRASES CORRECTAS

I'm moving to Tokyo for a year. I need to brush up on my Japanese. ☑
I'm moving to Tokyo for a year. I need to brush down my Japanese. ☐

1. Leo is the youngest in his class, but manages to keep up with his classmates. ☐
   Leo is the youngest in his class, but manages to keep on at his classmates. ☐

2. She's looking into how astronauts might travel to Mars one day. ☐
   She's looking onto how astronauts might travel to Mars one day. ☐

3. Sam has dived off his new project. He spent all weekend working on it. ☐
   Sam has dived into his new project. He spent all weekend working on it. ☐

4. The library was full of students swotting up on English grammar. ☐
   The library was full of students swotting out on English grammar. ☐

5. At the start of your presentation, lay out the main points you are going to discuss. ☐
   At the start of your presentation, lay on the main points you are going to discuss. ☐

Aa 20.4 COMPLETA LOS ESPACIOS PONIENDO LAS PALABRAS EN SU ORDEN CORRECTO

| the | work | out |

Nadia stayed up all night trying to __work__ __out__ __the__ answer to the equation.

| in | majoring | is |

1. Noah _____ _____ _____ international politics at college.

| start | to | over |

2. I kept making mistakes, so I decided _____ _____ _____ .

| space | focuses | on |

3. Patsy's research _____ _____ _____ travel.

| through | the | worked |

4. Fiona _____ _____ _____ problems in her code to fix the issues.

Aa 20.5 LEE EL ARTÍCULO Y ESCRIBE LOS PHRASAL VERBS SOBRE SUS DEFINICIONES

1
_____
enfrentarse a un reto de forma metódica

6
_____
presentar de manera clara

2
_____
pasar al punto siguiente

sum up
resumir el argumento

5
_____
prestar atención a

3
_____
contar para

4
_____
bajarle la nota a alguien

How to structure a presentation:
At the start of your presentation, **lay out** the main points you are going to discuss. Then, **move on to** presenting each of your arguments clearly and succinctly. **Focus on** being coherent and logical as you speak, making sure to emphasize all important points. At the end of your presentation, you should finish by **summing up** each of your conclusions. Include time for interaction with the audience and **work through** all questions calmly and confidently. Take care when writing your presentation, as you will be **marked down** for incorrect spelling and this will **count toward** your final assessment.

20.6 ESCUCHA EL AUDIO Y LUEGO NUMERA LAS IMÁGENES EN EL ORDEN EN QUE APARECEN

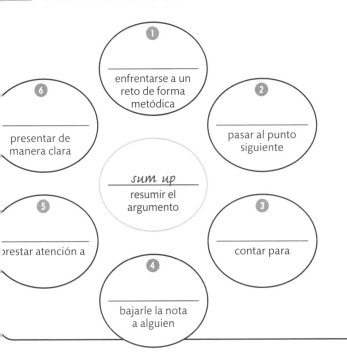

A ☐

B 1

C ☐

D ☐

E ☐

F ☐

G ☐

H ☐

21 En la escuela

21.1 ESCUELA

Ola dropped out of high school without any qualifications, but she went on to become a successful businesswoman.

drop out
abandonar la escuela o la universidad sin acabar los estudios

Miguel handed in his assignment five minutes before the deadline.

hand in (to)
entregar un trabajo a un profesor, dar algo a alguien con autoridad

The teacher handed out the worksheet to each member of the class.

hand out (to)
dar algo a cada miembro de un grupo, distribuir

The teacher wiped the notes off the board before Ed had finished copying them.

wipe off
retirar algo (con un trapo)

Schools break up in July in the UK. There is a six-week summer holiday.

break up (UK)
cerrar por vacaciones

Ramu's working on a new art project. It's a huge painting of New York.

work on
dedicar tiempo o esfuerzos a algo

When the class finished, Arun packed up his things and got ready to leave.

pack up
recoger tus cosas y colocarlas en una bolsa, mochila o caja

Good morning class. Please take out your books.

Now turn to page 25 and complete the exercises.

take out
sacar algo (de una bolsa o mochila)

turn to
abrir un libro por una página concreta

Ver también:
break up **3**, **15**, **29**, **38**   mess around **41**
take out **3**, **14**, **28**   turn to **13**, **45**, **50**   wipe off **14**

21.2 MAL COMPORTAMIENTO

You've spent too much time goofing off this semester, Jesse.

I will not stand for laziness. It's time you started working harder.

goof off (US)
perder el tiempo, no trabajar

not stand for
no tolerar, no dejar que alguien haga algo

The kids have been playing up all morning.

play up (UK)
hacer travesuras, portarse mal

Ffion is so naughty. She's always fooling around in class instead of paying attention.

fool around
hacer tonterías

Despite the teacher's warnings, the children carried on misbehaving.

carry on
continuar (haciendo algo)

The teacher told his students to stop messing around, and to do their work.

mess around
portarse mal, hacer algo que no deberías estar haciendo

Mateo and Juanita are very naughty, but Martina lets them get away with it.

get away with
hacer algo mal y quedar sin castigo

Rosie is very rude to her teachers. She's always answering back.

answer back
responder con mala educación (a un profesor o progenitor...)

Marco was furious about the broken window, but he let Gio and Carmen off with a warning.

let off (with)
no castigar a alguien o castigarle muy poco

Zosia told the children off when she saw the terrible mess they had made.

tell off
regañar a alguien por haber hecho alguna travesura

🔊

97

Aa 21.3 LEE LA FRASE Y MARCA EL SIGNIFICADO CORRECTO

Ramu's working on a new art project.
Ramu piensa en un proyecto de arte. ☐
Ramu dedica tiempo a un proyecto de arte. ☑
Ramu está interesado en un proyecto de arte. ☐

1 Schools break up in July in the UK.
Las escuelas abren en julio. ☐
Las escuelas organizan eventos en julio. ☐
Las escuelas cierran en julio. ☐

2 Marco let Gio and Carmen off with a warning.
Marco ha castigado a Gio y Carmen. ☐
Marco no ha castigado a Gio y Carmen. ☐
Marco ha hablado con Gio y Carmen. ☐

3 Zosia told the children off for the mess they had made.
Zosia felicitó a los niños. ☐
Zosia riñó a los niños. ☐
Zosia ayudó a los niños a poner orden. ☐

4 Rosie is always answering back to her teachers.
Rosie responde mal a sus maestros. ☐
Rosie responde educadamente a sus maestros. ☐
Rosie no responde a sus maestros. ☐

Aa 21.4 CONECTA LAS IMÁGENES CON LAS FRASES CORRECTAS

Miguel handed in his assignment just before the deadline.

1 Rosie is very rude. She's always answering back.

2 The teacher handed out the worksheet to each student.

3 After the class, Arun packed up his things and got ready to leave.

4 Ramu's working on a huge painting of New York.

21.5 ESCUCHA EL AUDIO Y MARCA LOS PHRASAL VERBS QUE APARECEN

tell off ☑	play up ☐	drop out ☐
1 tell off ☐	not stand for ☐	get away with ☐
2 hand in ☐	drop out ☐	take out ☐
3 carry on ☐	answer back ☐	drop out ☐
4 tell off ☐	take out ☐	play up ☐

21.6 ESCRIBE EL PHRASAL VERB CORRECTO AL LADO DE SU DEFINICIÓN

cerrar por vacaciones	=	*break up*
❶ dar algo a cada miembro de un grupo, distribuir	=	_____
❷ retirar algo (con un trapo)	=	_____
❸ no tolerar, no dejar que alguien haga algo	=	_____
❹ abandonar la escuela sin acabar los estudios	=	_____
❺ ir a una página concreta	=	_____

Aa **21.7 MIRA LAS IMÁGENES Y COMPLETA LAS FRASES CON PHRASAL VERBS DEL RECUADRO**

Ola ____*dropped out*____ of school, but went on to become a successful businesswoman.

❸ Despite the teacher's warnings, the children _____ misbehaving.

❶ Good morning class. Please_____ your books.

❹ You've spent too much time _____ this semester, Jesse.

❷ The kids have been _____ all morning.

❺ Mateo and Juanita are very naughty, but Martina lets them _____ it.

playing up	take out	goofing off	get away with	carried on	~~dropped out~~

22 En el trabajo

22.1 EMPEZAR Y ACABAR

I clock in **at 9am every morning.**

clock in
empezar a trabajar

I clock off **at 5pm every afternoon.**

clock off
acabar de trabajar

Despite the storm, the engineers soldiered on **and installed the new phone line.**

soldier on
*continuar intentando conseguir
algo a pesar de las dificultades*

Debbie took **the afternoon** off **so she could go to the dentist.**

take off
*dejar de trabajar un tiempo
determinado*

**I'm not feeling very well today,
so I'm going to** call in **sick.**

call in
llamar al lugar de trabajo

Steve gets off **work early on Fridays so he
can collect his children from school.**

get off
acabar de trabajar

◀))

22.2 REUNIONES

**Our manager was busy, so she had
to** call off **our meeting.**

call off
cancelar un acontecimiento

Let's talk over **all your designs
and make a decision.**

talk over
debatir

Angela meets up with **her colleagues
once a week to discuss all their
new ideas.**

meet up (with)
encontrarse con

I might be busy tomorrow, but let's
pencil in **a meeting anyway.**

pencil in
*acordar una fecha u hora, pero que
se puede cambiar más adelante*

◀))

Ver también:
call in **4**, **50**   get off **9**
take off **5**, **6**, **9**, **55**   talk over **36**

22.3 TRABAJAR

The applications for the new manager position are piling up. I'd better start looking through them.

pile up
aumentar hasta una cantidad imposible de gestionar

Fiona was struggling to finalize the company's accounts, but she kept plugging away at them.

plug away (at)
trabajar duro para conseguir algo complicado

Jennie's been slogging away trying to finish writing her presentation.

slog away (at)
trabajar duro durante mucho tiempo

Kamal's manager chased up the report, which was already a week late.

chase up
pedir algo a alguien (otra vez)

Ted used to be very proactive, but he's been slacking off lately.

slack off
eludir el trabajo duro

Ola is carrying out a survey about worker satisfaction.

carry out
completar una tarea

Gio has been on vacation for two weeks, so he has a lot of work to catch up on.

catch up on
hacer trabajo que no habías tenido tiempo de hacer antes

I've got lots to do! I need to knuckle down and get it finished.

knuckle down
empezar a trabajar muy duro

I've been very busy lately, but I have next week off work.

have off
dejar de trabajar un tiempo determinado

22.4 MIRA LAS IMÁGENES Y COMPLETA LAS FRASES CON PHRASAL VERBS DEL RECUADRO

Steve _____*gets off*_____ work early on Fridays so he can collect his children from school.

④ Our manager was busy, so she had to _____ our meeting.

① Ted used to be very proactive, but he's been _____ lately.

⑤ Jennie's been _____ trying to finish writing her presentation.

② I've got lots to do! I need to _____ and get it finished.

⑥ Kamal's manager _____ the report, which was already a week late.

③ Angela _____ her colleagues once a week to discuss all their new ideas.

⑦ I _____ at 9am every morning.

call off	chased up	~~gets off~~	slacking off	clock in
	knuckle down	meets up with		slogging away

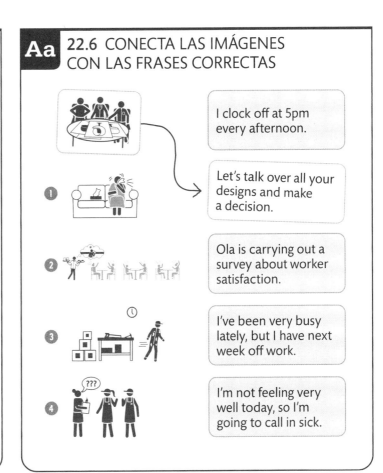

22.5 ESCUCHA EL AUDIO Y MARCA LOS PHRASAL VERBS QUE APARECEN

A call in ☐

B knuckle down ☐

C slog away at ☑

D have off ☐

E call off ☐

F chase up ☐

G meet up with ☐

H carry out ☐

I talk over ☐

Aa 22.6 CONECTA LAS IMÁGENES CON LAS FRASES CORRECTAS

I clock off at 5pm every afternoon.

Let's talk over all your designs and make a decision.

Ola is carrying out a survey about worker satisfaction.

I've been very busy lately, but I have next week off work.

I'm not feeling very well today, so I'm going to call in sick.

Aa 22.7 VUELVE A ESCRIBIR LAS FRASES CORRIGIENDO LOS ERRORES

Gio has been on vacation for two weeks, so he has a lot of work to **throw up on**.

Gio has been on vacation for two weeks, so he has a lot of work to catch up on.

1 The applications for the new manager position are **piling over**. I'd better start looking through them.

---

2 Fiona was struggling to finalize the company's accounts, but she kept **switching away** at them.

---

3 Debbie **took** the afternoon **down** so she could go to the dentist.

---

4 Despite the storm, the engineers **marched on** and installed the new phone line.

---

23 Trayectoria profesional

23.1 TRAYECTORIA PROFESIONAL

After 35 years running his own company, Robert is standing down and retiring.

stand down
abandonar una profesión o cargo importante

His daughter Jess is taking over the family business.

take over
responsabilizarse de una empresa o un cargo

Katie has been a therapist for 20 years, so she has a lot of experience to draw on.

draw on
sacar partido de la experiencia

Olivia is trying to get into journalism. She's just started an internship at a radio station.

get into
participar en algo, empezar una profesión

If I ever lose my job at the bank, I'll always have my cooking skills to fall back on.

fall back on
utilizar habilidades que ya tienes (cuando algo va mal)

When he left school, Paul set out to become a millionaire by the time he reached 30.

set out
empezar a hacer algo con un objetivo específico en mente

Carolina went on a training course to help her get ahead at work.

get ahead (at)
mejorar tu cargo en el trabajo

I went back to my job as a mechanic when my children started school.

go back to
volver al trabajo tras un parón

Joanna is winding down her business to take a job managing a large hotel.

wind down
cerrar de manera gradual

Chad just finished his degree and is applying for jobs in the media.

applying for
presentarse para un puesto de trabajo

Ver también:
get into **31**   put off **55**   set out **35, 53**
wind down **31**

Thanks to his impressive portfolio, Elliot walked into a job with a leading fashion designer.

walk into
encontrar empleo con facilidad

Marvin has become such a successful tennis player that he's branching out into coaching younger players.

branch out (into)
empezar a hacer algo diferente (pero relacionado)

Ken's going to burn himself out if he keeps working 16 hours a day.

burn out
acabar extenuado por trabajar demasiado

We have chosen Diana to head up our new sales department.

head up
dirigir, estar al cargo de un departamento u organización

I thought I wanted to be a lawyer, but the workload put me off.

put off
hacer que a alguien no le guste una persona o una cosa

Femi has thrown himself into his new job at the hair salon. He loves it!

throw (oneself) into
empezar a hacer algo con mucho entusiasmo

Naina is planning to go into teaching when she finishes university.

go into
empezar una profesión concreta

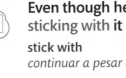

Even though he doesn't like his job, Tom is sticking with it until he gets promoted.

stick with
continuar a pesar de las dificultades

Brian has started selling umbrellas in his store to cash in on the recent terrible weather.

cash in on
aprovecharse de una situación para ganar dinero

23.2 ESCUCHA EL AUDIO Y CONECTA LAS IMÁGENES CON LOS PHRASAL VERBS CORRECTOS

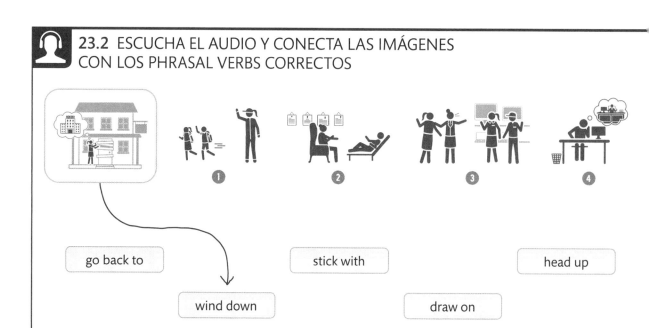

go back to

stick with

head up

wind down

draw on

Aa 23.3 LEE LA FRASE Y MARCA EL SIGNIFICADO CORRECTO

Femi has thrown himself into his new job.

Femi está nervioso por su nuevo trabajo. ☐

Femi está entusiasmado con su trabajo. ☑

A Femi no le gusta su nuevo trabajo. ☐

① Elliot walked into a job with a fashion designer.

Elliot va a pie al trabajo. ☐

Fue fácil para Elliot encontrar empleo. ☐

Elliot llegó tarde al trabajo. ☐

② Katie has a lot of experience to draw on.

Katie és una artista. ☐

Katie saca partido de su experiencia. ☐

Katie quiere acumular más experiencia. ☐

③ Naina is planning to go into teaching.

Naina planea reunirse con su profesora. ☐

Naina planea convertirse en profesora. ☐

Naina planea ir a la escuela. ☐

④ I went back to my job as a mechanic.

He ido a ver al mecánico. ☐

He vuelto a trabajar. ☐

Quiero ser mecánico. ☐

⑤ Diana heads up our new sales department.

Diana dirige el nuevo departamento. ☐

Diana fundó el nuevo departamento. ☐

A Diana no le gusta el nuevo departamento. ☐

⑥ Chad is applying for jobs in the media.

Chad no está buscando empleo. ☐

Chad trabaja en comunicación. ☐

Chad busca empleo en comunicación. ☐

⑦ Olivia is trying to get into journalism.

Olivia intenta convertirse en periodista. ☐

Olivia intenta reunirse con un periodista. ☐

Olivia es periodista. ☐

23.4 ESCRIBE EL PHRASAL VERB CORRECTO AL LADO DE SU DEFINICIÓN, COMPLETANDO LAS LETRAS QUE FALTAN

| abandonar una profesión o cargo importante | = | s t a n d   d o w n |

1 continuar a pesar de las dificultades = s _ _ _ _   w _ _ _

2 presentarse para un puesto de trabajo = a _ _ _ _   f _ _

3 responsabilizarse de una empresa o cargo = t _ _ _   o _ _ _

4 volver a un trabajo tras un parón = g _   b _ _ _   t _

5 cerrar de manera gradual = w _ _ _   d _ _ _

Aa **23.5** ESCRIBE LOS PHRASAL VERBS DEL RECUADRO BAJO LAS DEFINICIONES CORRECTAS

| mejorar tu cargo en el trabajo
get ahead (at) |

4 hacer que a alguien no le guste una persona o una cosa

_____

1 participar en algo, empezar una profesión

_____

5 aprovecharse de una situación para ganar dinero

_____

2 acabar extenuado por trabajar demasiado

_____

6 utilizar habilidades que ya tienes (cuando algo va mal)

_____

3 empezar a hacer algo diferente (pero relacionado)

_____

7 empezar a hacer algo con un objetivo específico en mente

_____

| cash in on   set out   branch out (into)   put off   burn out |
| get into   ~~get ahead (at)~~   fall back on |

24 Empresa

24.1 EMPRESA

We are proud to announce that our two banks are entering into a partnership.

enter into
establecer una relación (comercial)

Katie's trying to drum up interest in her café by offering free samples of her cakes.

drum up
aumentar el apoyo por algo

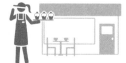

Marco's garden center is doing well. It turns over almost $250,000 a year.

turn over
(una empresa) ganar un dinero en un período concreto de tiempo

Alan's sportswear company profited from the cold weather earlier this year.

profit from
sacar provecho de una situación

The board has finally come to a decision about the new logo for the company.

come to
llegar a, alcanzar (una decisión)

Chrissie has just started up her own hair salon. It opened last week.

start up
abrir una empresa

Mario's gas station has just gone under. It had been struggling for a long time.

go under
caer en bancarrota

Ellie's company deals in antiques. She sells pieces from all over the world.

deal in
comprar y vender bienes

Elsa's tired of running her own business. She's decided to sell up.

sell up
vender una empresa

The bank agreed to write off the debt, saving Ethan's company from bankruptcy.

write off
cancelar una deuda

Ver también:
come to **14**   open up **45**

All of the banks in our town have closed down. Everyone's using online banking.

close down
cerrar de manera permanente

My plans to expand my business fell through when the bank refused to lend me enough money.

fall through
no ocurrir

Gemma has bought out all the other partners. She now owns the whole company.

buy out
comprar la parte de alguien de una empresa

Rita's company sells furniture, but farms out all of its manufacturing to other people.

farm out (to)
delegar parte de tu trabajo a personas que no trabajan en tu empresa

Our business is growing, so we are taking on more staff.

take on
contratar

We need the CEO to sign off on this important decision.

sign off on
aprobar algo de manera oficial

A new bookstore is opening up in our neighborhood.

open up
abrir por primera vez

Al's store is selling off a lot of its stock. There are some great bargains there.

sell off
vender algo rápido a precio reducido

The company is facing difficulties. We may need to lay off some staff.

lay off
despedir a alguien

Could you draw up a contract for our new clients?

draw up
redactar un contrato

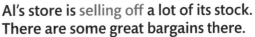

Aa 24.2 CONECTA LAS IMÁGENES CON LAS FRASES CORRECTAS

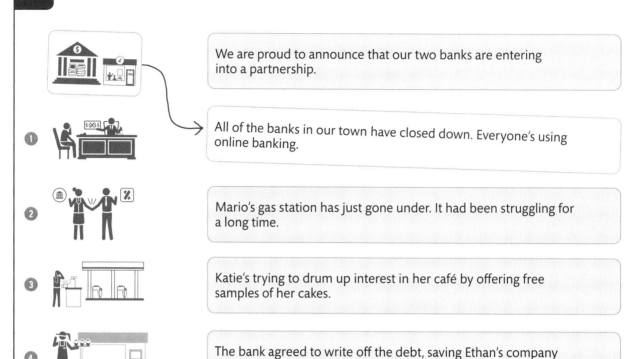

We are proud to announce that our two banks are entering into a partnership.

All of the banks in our town have closed down. Everyone's using online banking.

Mario's gas station has just gone under. It had been struggling for a long time.

Katie's trying to drum up interest in her café by offering free samples of her cakes.

The bank agreed to write off the debt, saving Ethan's company from bankruptcy.

Aa 24.3 TACHA LAS PALABRAS INCORRECTAS DE CADA FRASE

Elsa's tired of running her own business. She's decided to ~~trade~~ / sell / ~~walk~~ up.

1 Marco's garden center is doing well. It turns down / over / forward almost $250,000 a year.

2 We need the CEO to sign / mark / stamp off on this important decision.

3 The board has finally arrived / reached / come to a decision about the new logo for the company.

4 Ellie's company deals on / in / for antiques. She sells pieces from all over the world.

5 Could you sketch / draw / paint up a contract for our new clients?

6 The company is facing difficulties. We may need to lay off / out / down some staff.

24.4 ESCUCHA EL AUDIO Y MARCA LOS PHRASAL VERBS QUE APARECEN

| write off | ☑ | sell off | ☐ | take on | ☐ |

1. close down ☐ · fall through ☐ · start up ☐
2. gone under ☐ · buy out ☐ · come to ☐
3. sign off ☐ · draw up ☐ · lay off ☐
4. take on ☐ · open up ☐ · drum up ☐
5. enter into ☐ · fall through ☐ · fall from ☐
6. walk up ☐ · farm out to ☐ · profit from ☐

Aa 24.5 COMPLETA LOS ESPACIOS CON LOS PHRASAL VERBS DEL RECUADRO

Could you __*draw up*__ a contract for our new clients?

opening up

1. Our business is growing, so we are _____ more staff.

bought out

2. A new bookstore is _____ in our neighborhood.

selling off

3. Chrissie has just _____ her own hair salon. It opened last week.

taking on

4. Gemma has _____ all the other partners.

~~draw up~~

5. Al's store is _____ a lot of its stock.

profited from

6. Alan's sportswear company _____ the cold weather.

started up

25 Números y cantidades

25.1 NÚMEROS Y CANTIDADES

Katie's bills have been stacking **up. She's in a lot of debt now.**

stack up
aumentar en número o cantidad

The temperature varies a bit in the summer, but it averages **out at about 25°C.**

average out (at)
dar como resultado un promedio de

The price for our cruise was going to be $1,207, but the travel agent agreed to round **it** down **to $1,200.**

round down (to)
redondear a una cifra inferior (normalmente acabada en cero)

We estimated the cost of the project to be £14,900, but rounded **it** up **to the nearest thousand.**

round up (to)
redondear a una cifra superior (normalmente acabada en cero)

The kids are counting down **the days before we go camping.**

count down
contar el tiempo que falta para que pase algo

Alfie counted out **the money he owed me and placed it on the table.**

count out
contar cosas una por una y colocarlas en algún sitio

The company's share price has been falling, but it's finally starting to bottom out.

bottom out
dejar de empeorar, llegar a su punto mínimo

After falling dramatically in May, the price of gold has evened out **over the past two months.**

even out
equilibrarse, contener menos diferencias o irregularidades

The number of people buying clothes online shot up **last year.**

shoot up
aumentar de manera importante

Over the last six months, it has started to level out.

level out
equilibrarse, dejar de subir o bajar

Ver también:
add up **14**, **41**   take away **30**, **55**

The coach divided **the children**
up into two equal teams.

divide up (into)
separar en grupos,
partes o secciones

If you want to set yourself a budget,
start by adding up **all your**
monthly expenses.

add up
calcular el total

Renovating a house is very expensive.
The cost soon mounts up.

mount up
aumentar en número o
cantidad de forma gradual

Shreya counted up **the number of**
people wanting coffee and went
to make some.

count up
sumar cosas o personas que
forman parte de un grupo

When Georgia was paying her check,
she added on **a 20% tip.**

add on
añadir una cosa o cantidad
adicional a algo

25.2 OPERACIONES MATEMÁTICAS

If you add **20 and 4 together,**
you get 24.

$20+4=24$

add together
calcular el total de dos
o más números

The teacher asked what's left when you
take 4 away from 20.

$20-4=$
16

take away (from)
restar

For the next question, the class
had to multiply 20 by 4.

multiply by
multiplicar por

$20\times4=80$

Does anyone know what
20 divided by 4 equals?

$20\div4=$
5

divide by
dividir por

Aa 25.3 MARCA LAS FRASES CORRECTAS

The kids are counting down the days before we go camping. ✓
The kids are counting below the days before we go camping. ☐

1. The number of people buying clothes online shot up last year. ☐
   The number of people buying clothes online bought up last year. ☐

2. The coach divided the children above into two equal teams. ☐
   The coach divided the children up into two equal teams. ☐

3. Shreya counted up the number of people wanting coffee and went to make some. ☐
   Shreya counted on the number of people wanting coffee and went to make some. ☐

4. When Georgia was paying her check, she added on a 20% tip. ☐
   When Georgia was paying her check, she divided on a 20% tip. ☐

25.4 ESCUCHA EL AUDIO Y LUEGO NUMERA LAS IMÁGENES EN EL ORDEN EN QUE APARECEN

A ☐

B 1

C ☐

D ☐

E ☐

F ☐

25.5 VUELVE A ESCRIBIR LAS FRASES CORRIGIENDO LOS ERRORES

> Alfie **counted of** the money he owed me and placed it on the table.
>
> *Alfie counted out the money he owed me and placed it on the table.*

1 Katie's bills have been **stacking over**. She's in a lot of debt now.

_____

2 The company's share price has been falling, but it's finally starting to **ground out**.

_____

3 The temperature varies a bit in the summer, but it **averages in at** about 25°C.

_____

4 We estimated the cost of the project to be £14,900, but **mounted** it **up to** the nearest thousand.

_____

5 If you want to set yourself a budget, start by **scoring up** all your monthly expenses.

_____

Aa **25.6** ESCRIBE EL PHRASAL VERB CORRECTO AL LADO DE SU DEFINICIÓN

aumentar en número o cantidad de manera gradual	=	*mount up*
1 contar el tiempo que falta para que pase algo	=	_____
2 calcular el total	=	_____
3 dar como resultado un promedio de	=	_____
4 equilibrarse, dejar de subir o bajar	=	_____
5 contar cosas una por una y colocarlas en algún sitio	=	_____
6 dejar de empeorar, llegar a su punto mínimo	=	_____

level out   count out   count down   add up   ~~mount up~~   average out (at)   bottom out

26 Éxito y fracaso

26.1 ÉXITO

Nia **built on** her experience working at a hotel to set up her own guesthouse.

build on
aprovechar el conocimiento, experiencia o éxito para cosechar más éxitos

Clive **muddled through** the interview without any preparation. He was shocked when he got the job.

muddle through
conseguir realizar algo a pesar de no tener planes o conocimientos

When I didn't get into college, I started my own successful business. Everything **worked out** in the end!

work out
obtener un resultado positivo

I know these results are disappointing, but keep working and you will **win out** eventually.

win out
conseguir algo tras un período de dificultades

Anita's hard work has **paid off**. The dress looks beautiful.

pay off
dar un beneficio tras invertir tiempo o dinero

I never imagined James would be so great playing Hamlet, but he really **carried** it **off**.

carry off
tener éxito en algo de forma imprevista

The Scottish team **pulled off** an amazing victory, scoring two goals in the last four minutes.

pull off
triunfar (pese a las dificultades)

Maria's dream of becoming famous finally **came off** when her song became a huge summer hit.

come off
triunfar (un plan)

Marco did not study at all for the English exam but somehow **scraped by**.

scrape by
conseguir algo por los pelos

Kwase **sailed through** his driving test. He didn't make any mistakes.

sail through
conseguir algo con facilidad

🔊

Ver también:
come off **6**, **52**   give up **55**   pay off **14**
run into **14**   work out **20**, **33**

26.2 FRACASO

Marcello tried to fix the washing machine, but he has given up.

give up
dejar de intentar conseguir algo

Many smaller stores have lost out **since the supermarket opened in town.**

lose out (to)
ser derrotado

Simon's campaign ran into **difficulties when he was accused of lying.**

run into
empezar a experimentar algo negativo

The decorators have screwed up **this job! We won't use them again.**

screw up
provocar un lío (informal)

26.3 CAUSAS DE ÉXITOS Y FRACASOS

The future success of our company rides on **us winning this contract.**

ride on
depender de

When accepting the award, Carla put **her success** down to **hard work.**

put down to
atribuir cosas a un motivo concreto

Having supportive parents really contributed to **my success.**

contribute to
ayudar a conseguir algo

My teachers told me I'd never amount to **anything, but now I'm a lawyer.**

amount to
llegar a ser (a menudo usado en negativo)

When Al saw how many people were making money by selling things online, he decided to get in on **it.**

get in on
implicarse en una actividad fructífera

Aa 26.4 CONECTA LAS DEFINICIONES CON LOS PHRASAL VERBS CORRECTOS

triunfar (un plan)	win out
① conseguir algo por los pelos	sail through
② tener éxito en algo de forma imprevista	come off
③ triunfar tras las dificultades	carry off
④ conseguir algo con facilidad	run into
⑤ empezar a experimentar algo negativo	screw up
⑥ dejar de intentar conseguir algo	scrape by
⑦ provocar un lío	give up

triunfar (un plan) → come off

26.5 ESCUCHA EL AUDIO Y MARCA LOS PHRASAL VERBS QUE APARECEN

scrape by ☑ give up ☐

① screw up ☐   put down to ☐

② carry off ☐   ride on ☐

③ win out ☐   win over ☐

④ come off ☐   come up ☐

⑤ run into ☐   run off ☐

26.6 MARCA LAS FRASES CORRECTAS

When accepting the award, Carla put her success down to hard work. ☑
When accepting the award, Carla put her success up to hard work. ☐

1. My teachers told me I'd never add up to anything, but now I'm a lawyer. ☐
My teachers told me I'd never amount to anything, but now I'm a lawyer. ☐

2. Anita's hard work has paid up. The dress looks beautiful. ☐
Anita's hard work has paid off. The dress looks beautiful. ☐

3. Many smaller stores have lost out since the supermarket opened in town. ☐
Many smaller stores have closed out since the supermarket opened in town. ☐

4. Nia looked on her experience working at a hotel to set up her own guesthouse. ☐
Nia built on her experience working at a hotel to set up her own guesthouse. ☐

5. Having supportive parents really attributed to my success. ☐
Having supportive parents really contributed to my success. ☐

Aa 26.7 VUELVE A ESCRIBIR LAS FRASES CORRIGIENDO LOS ERRORES

The future success of our company **drives on** us winning this contract.
The future success of our company rides on us winning this contract.

1. Clive **muddled on** the interview without any preparation. He was shocked when he got the job.

2. When I didn't get into college, I started my own successful business. Everything **worked up** in the end!

3. The Scottish team **pushed off** an amazing victory, scoring two goals in the last four minutes.

4. When Al saw how many people were making money by selling things online, he decided to **get out on** it.

5. Kwase **sailed into** his driving test. He didn't make any mistakes.

27 En casa

27.1 PHRASAL VERBS CON "LOCK"

Clive makes sure that he locks his tools away in his shed.

lock away
guardar algo y cerrar la puerta con llave

When Ben got home, he realized that he'd forgotten his keys and was locked out.

lock out
evitar que entre nadie cerrando la puerta con llave

The janitor didn't notice Alex when he locked the doors. He accidentally locked him in.

lock in
evitar que alguien salga cerrando la puerta con llave

27.3 LUCES Y ELECTRODOMÉSTICOS

Did you leave the lights on when you left the house?

leave on
dejar encendido

The lights in the house went out, so Clara lit some candles.

go out
(luces) dejar de brillar

It was a very hot day, so Les put the fan on.

put on (UK)
poner en marcha un electrodoméstico

Andy blew the candles out before going to bed.

blow out
apagar una vela soplando

If you're bored, turn on the television. There's a good movie on tonight.

turn on
poner algo en funcionamiento

Make sure you turn the television off before going to bed.

turn off
desconectar algo

Ver también:
come on **52**, **56**   go off **3**, **8**, **30**, **35**   go out **3**, **5**, **54**
put on **6**, **41**, **55**   turn off **9**   turn on **1**   turn up **1**, **4**

27.2 MUDANZAS

Pete's new neighbors moved in last weekend.

move in(to)
empezar a vivir en otra casa

We finally sold our house. We're moving out today.

move out (of)
dejar de vivir en tu vieja casa de antes y mudarte a otra

My parents have decided to move away and live in the country.

move away
ir a vivir a una zona diferente

Jools has settled into his new apartment very quickly.

settle in(to)
acostumbrarse a vivir en un sitio nuevo

When Elsa heard her favorite song on the radio, she turned up the volume and began dancing.

turn up
subir el volumen (o la potencia) de un aparato

Paula's neighbor asked her to turn her stereo down because it was too loud.

turn down
bajar el volumen (o la potencia) de un aparato

Cassie thought her computer was broken until she realized that she hadn't plugged it in.

plug in(to)
enchufar un electrodoméstico

The street lights come on at dusk, when the sun sets.

come on
ponerse a funcionar (automáticamente)

The street lights go off at dawn, when the sun rises.

go off
dejar de funcionar (automáticamente)

Aa 27.4 MIRA LAS IMÁGENES Y COMPLETA LAS FRASES CON PHRASAL VERBS DEL RECUADRO

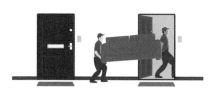

Pete's new neighbors _____*moved in*_____ last weekend.

1 If you're bored, _____ the television. There's a good movie on tonight.

2 When Ben got home, he realized that he'd forgotten his keys and was _____ .

3 My parents have decided to _____ and live in the country.

4 When Elsa heard her favorite song on the radio, she _____ the volume.

5 The street lights _____ at dusk, when the sun sets.

6 The lights in the house _____ , so Clara lit some candles.

7 We finally sold our house. We're _____ _____ today.

moving out	come on	turn on	move away
locked out	~~moved in~~	turned up	went out

Aa 27.5 CONECTA LOS PHRASAL VERBS CON SUS CONTRARIOS

put on — turn off

1. come on — go off

2. move out → turn off

3. lock in — move in

4. turn off — turn down

5. turn up — lock out

(Opciones: go off, turn on, turn off, move in, turn down, lock out)

27.6 ESCUCHA EL AUDIO Y LUEGO NUMERA LAS IMÁGENES EN EL ORDEN EN QUE APARECEN

A ☐   B 1

C ☐   D ☐

E ☐   F ☐

Aa 27.7 ESCRIBE EL PHRASAL VERB CORRECTO AL LADO DE SU DEFINICIÓN

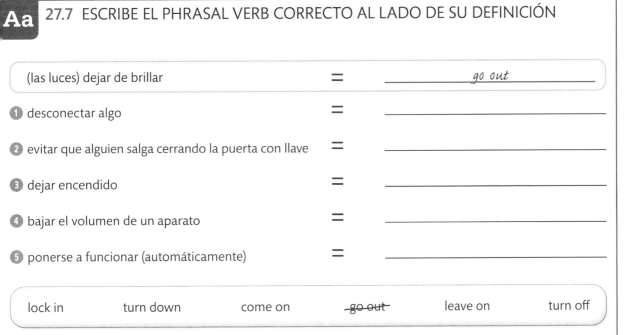

(las luces) dejar de brillar = *go out*

1. desconectar algo = _____

2. evitar que alguien salga cerrando la puerta con llave = _____

3. dejar encendido = _____

4. bajar el volumen de un aparato = _____

5. ponerse a funcionar (automáticamente) = _____

lock in   turn down   come on   ~~go out~~   leave on   turn off

28.1 LIMPIAR

We need to tidy up before the guests arrive.

tidy up
volver a dejarlo todo en orden

Elliot's dad told him to clear away all his toys.

clear away
volver a colocar las cosas en el sitio adecuado

Jason told me to mop up the water that I'd spilled on the floor.

mop up
secar una superficie con una mopa

This room is a mess! Pick up all these clothes!

pick up
recoger algo del suelo

If the chicken smells bad, you should throw it away.

throw away
desechar, tirar a la basura

When Ella cooks dinner, her boyfriend washes up the dishes.

wash up (UK)
fregar los platos

After painting the living room, Paul and Sally put all the furniture back.

put back
devolver un objeto a su lugar original

It was a sunny morning, so Ian hung his washing out to dry.

hang out
tender la colada para que se seque

There was a lot of mess to clean up after the party.

clean up
volver a dejarlo todo en orden

We all pitched in to get it finished more quickly.

pitch in
unirse, ayudar a otros a hacer algo

Ver también:
cut back **14**   hang out **5**   pick up **9**, **10**, **11**, **31**, **38**   pull up **9**
put up **35**   take out **3**, **14**, **21**   throw away **31**

We cleared out the garage this weekend. There was so much junk in there!

clear out
retirar todas las cosas innecesarias de una habitación o edificio

---

I wipe down the table each evening after we've eaten.

wipe down
limpiar una superficie con un trapo

On Tuesday mornings, I take the trash out.

take out
sacar algo fuera

Nousha's room looked much nicer after she'd put up some pictures.

put up
colgar algo en una pared

Karl swept up the trash from the party and put it into bags.

sweep up
limpiar el suelo con una escoba

28.2 JARDÍN

The tree in our backyard died, so we had to chop it down.

chop down
talar un árbol

The hedge in Doug's yard was getting too big, so he cut it back.

cut back
podar parte de las ramas de un árbol, arbusto o seto

I'm digging up the lavender bushes so I can move them to a different part of the garden.

dig up
sacar una planta del suelo cavando a su alrededor y por debajo

---

Paul spent the whole afternoon pulling up weeds. His yard was full of them.

pull up
arrancar una planta del suelo tirando de ella

After finishing the gardening, Scott put his tools away.

put away
devolver un objeto a su lugar adecuado

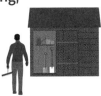

Aa 28.3 CONECTA LAS DEFINICIONES CON LOS PHRASAL VERBS CORRECTOS

recoger algo del suelo	pull up
1 devolver un objeto a su lugar original	chop down
2 talar un árbol	pick up
3 unirse, ayudar a otros a hacer algo	take out
4 arrancar una planta del suelo tirando de ella	wash up
5 sacar algo fuera	put back
6 retirar todas las cosas innecesarias de una habitación	pitch in
7 fregar los platos	clear out

Aa 28.4 TACHA LAS PALABRAS INCORRECTAS DE CADA FRASE

Elliot's dad told him to clear ~~up~~ / away / ~~out~~ all his toys.

1 Nousha's room looked much nicer after she'd put up / in / on some pictures.

2 Paul spent the whole afternoon pulling on / in / up weeds.

3 Karl swept down / over / up the trash from the party and put it into bags.

4 After finishing the gardening, Scott put his tools up / away / out.

5 Jason told me to mop up / around / over the water that I'd spilled on the floor.

28.5 ESCUCHA EL AUDIO Y COMPLETA LAS FRASES QUE DESCRIBEN LAS IMÁGENES

This room is a mess! _____Pick up_____ all these clothes!

③ I _____ the table each evening after we've eaten.

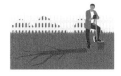

① The tree in our backyard died, so we had to _____ .

④ We need to _____ before the guests arrive.

② I'm _____ the lavender bushes so I can move them to a different part of the garden.

⑤ The hedge in Doug's yard was getting too big, so he _____.

Aa ## 28.6 VUELVE A ESCRIBIR LAS FRASES CORRIGIENDO LOS ERRORES

We all **pitched out** to get it finished quickly.
We all pitched in to get it finished quickly.

① On Tuesday mornings, I **take** the trash **off**.

_____

② If the chicken smells bad, **throw** it **over**.

_____

③ Ian **hung** his washing **in** to dry.

_____

④ We **cleared over** the garage this weekend.

_____

⑤ There was a mess to **clean on** after the party.

_____

127

29.1 COCINA

Patrick broke up the chocolate before adding it to the cake mixture.

break up
separar algo en partes más pequeñas

Nadiya left the cherry pie on the windowsill to cool down.

cool down
enfriar, enfriarse

I always measure out all of my ingredients before trying a new recipe.

measure out
pesar o tomar una cantidad concreta

You should mix in the eggs and milk with the other ingredients.

mix in
mezclar (con más ingredientes)

My sister can whip up a tasty meal in minutes from just a few ingredients.

whip up
preparar (una comida) rápido

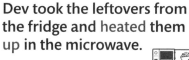

Before serving the curry I made sure to fish out any bones.

fish out
retirar de un líquido

The sauce boiled over, leaving a mess on the stove top.

boil over
rebosar por el borde de un recipiente (durante la cocción)

Dev took the leftovers from the fridge and heated them up in the microwave.

heat up
calentar

My breakfast typically consists of bread and cheese, served with coffee.

consist of
estar compuesto por

We managed to fill up three jars with the cookies we'd baked.

fill up
llenar un recipiente hasta el borde

Ver también:
break up **3**, **15**, **21**, **38**
cool down **11**

29.2 PREPARAR UNA RECETA

RECIPE

CHICKEN CASSEROLE

INGREDIENTS

2 onions
3 carrots
5 potatoes
2 chicken thighs
1 pint vegetable stock
Chopped parsley (to garnish)

SERVES: 4

PREP TIME: 15 minutes

COOK TIME: 30 minutes

METHOD

1. Start by **chopping up** some onions, carrots, and potatoes, then **set** them **aside** for later.

2. Fry the meat on a medium heat for 10 minutes (you may want to **cut off** any extra fat from the meat).

3. **Pour in** the stock, add the vegetables, and boil for 20 minutes.

4. **Finish off** the stew by adding chopped parsley.

Note: To make a vegetarian version, **leave out** the meat and use mushrooms instead.

Start by chopping up some onions, carrots, and potatoes.

chop up
cortar en trozos pequeños

After you've chopped the vegetables, set them aside for later.

set aside
reservar algo para más tarde

I always cut off the fat from the meat before cooking it.

cut off
separar algo de una pieza más grande

When the meat is cooked, pour in the stock.

pour in
añadir un líquido

Finish off the stew by adding chopped parsley.

finish off
completar

To make a vegetarian version, leave out the meat and use mushrooms instead.

leave out
excluir, no incluir

Aa 29.3 COMPLETA LOS ESPACIOS CON LOS PHRASAL VERBS DEL RECUADRO

You should _____*mix in*_____ the eggs and milk with the other ingredients.

1 I always _____ the fat from the meat before cooking it.

2 My breakfast typically _____ bread and cheese, served with coffee.

3 Nadiya left the cherry pie on the windowsill to _____.

4 Before serving the curry I made sure to _____ any bones.

5 My sister can _____ a tasty meal in minutes from just a few ingredients.

cool down   ~~mix in~~   cut off   whip up   fish out   consists of

29.4 ESCUCHA EL AUDIO Y MARCA LOS PHRASAL VERBS QUE APARECEN

measure out ✓
measure over ☐

1 chop off ☐
chop up ☐

2 set apart ☐
set aside ☐

3 cut off ☐
cut away ☐

4 mix up ☐
mix in ☐

5 pour in ☐
pour over ☐

6 finish off ☐
finish up ☐

7 fish out ☐
fish for ☐

8 cool off ☐
cool down ☐

9 leave out ☐
leave in ☐

Aa 29.5 CONECTA LAS IMÁGENES CON LAS FRASES CORRECTAS

The sauce boiled over, leaving a mess on the stove top.

Dev took the leftovers from the fridge and heated them up in the microwave.

1

I always measure out all of my ingredients before trying a new recipe.

2

Patrick broke up the chocolate before adding it to the cake mixture.

3

We managed to fill up three jars with the cookies we'd baked.

4

My sister can whip up a tasty meal in minutes from just a few ingredients.

5

⚙ 29.6 VUELVE A ESCRIBIR LAS FRASES CORRIGIENDO LOS ERRORES

Start by **chopping ups** onions and carrots.
Start by chopping up onions and carrots.

1 After chopping the vegetables, **set** them **beside**.

_____

2 **Cut on** the fat from the meat before cooking it.

_____

3 When the meat is cooked, **pour up** the stock.

_____

4 **Mix over** the eggs with the other ingredients.

_____

5 **Finish in** the stew by adding chopped parsley.

_____

6 Before serving, make sure to **fish on** any bones.

_____

7 For a vegetarian version, **leave down** the meat.

_____

30 Comida y bebida

30.1 COMIDA

Rosa served up a wonderful seafood dish.

serve up
servir comida a otros

Martin's grandmother told him he could only have dessert if he ate up all his vegetables.

eat up
comerte todo de algo

Selma and Roy prefer to eat in. It's much cheaper than going to a restaurant.

eat in
comer en casa

That fish really didn't agree with me. I have a terrible stomachache.

not agree with
sentar mal

I think this milk has gone off. It smells terrible.

go off (UK)
echarse a perder algún alimento o bebida

Apple pie and ice cream go together perfectly.

go together
saber o tener mejor aspecto juntos

Our restaurant can cater for about 100 customers at a time.

cater for
servir a

30.2 BEBIDA

After the wedding, we all drank to the bride and groom.

drink to
brindar por alguien o algo

The café was about to close, so we drank up and got ready to leave.

drink up
beberse algo del todo

Ver también:
break off **49**   go off **8**, **27**, **35**
run out (of) **15**   take away **25**, **55**

I was going to make a lasagna, but we've run out of pasta.

Why don't we eat out for a change? We could go to that new Italian restaurant instead.

run out (of)
gastar todo de algo, no quedar más de algo

eat out
comer en un bar o un restaurante, no comer en casa

Daniel broke off a piece of bread and dipped it in the olive oil.

break off
separar una parte pequeña de algo de una pieza más grande

Lisa shared out the chocolates, giving the children two each.

share out
servir a cada persona la misma cantidad de algo

Greg was so hungry that he polished off the entire cake.

polish off
comérselo o bebérselo todo

After a long day at the beach, my kids wolfed down their dinner.

wolf down
comérselo todo muy rápidamente

Paul and Sarah ordered two hamburgers and sodas to take away.

take away (UK)
comprar comida para llevar

This cake is delicious, but it could do without all the cream on top.

do without
ser mejor sin

I washed down my pizza with a cold drink.

wash down
beber algo después de comer (informal)

Your mug's almost empty, Peter. Would you like me to top it up?

top up
rellenar una copa o vaso medio vacíos

Aa 30.3 CONECTA LOS PRINCIPIOS DE LAS FRASES CON LOS FINALES CORRECTOS

Greg was so hungry that — he polished off the entire cake.

we all drank to the bride and groom.

1. I washed down my pizza

giving the children two each.

2. Our restaurant can cater for

3. After the wedding,

but we've run out of pasta.

4. Lisa shared out the chocolates,

about 100 customers at a time.

5. I was going to make a lasagna,

with a cold drink.

Aa 30.4 TACHA LAS PALABRAS INCORRECTAS DE CADA FRASE

After the wedding, we all drank ~~on~~ / to / ~~over~~ the bride and groom.

1. Paul and Sarah ordered two hamburgers and sodas to take **away** / **off** / **with**.

2. The café was about to close, so we drank **down** / **in** / **up** and got ready to leave.

3.  I washed **up** / **down** / **in** my pizza with a cold drink.

4. After a long day at the beach, my kids wolfed **out** / **down** / **on** their dinner.

5.  Daniel broke **over** / **off** / **down** a piece of bread and dipped it in the olive oil.

30.5 ESCUCHA EL AUDIO Y MARCA LOS PHRASAL VERBS QUE APARECEN

serve up ☑
serve over ☐

① run out of ☐
   run down ☐

② go on ☐
   go off ☐

③ eat up ☐
   eat down ☐

④ wash down ☐
   wash up ☐

⑤ go together ☐
   go with ☐

Aa 30.6 ESCRIBE EL PHRASAL VERB CORRECTO AL LADO DE SU DEFINICIÓN, COMPLETANDO LAS LETRAS QUE FALTAN

| comérselo o bebérselo todo | = | p o l i s h   o f f |

① no comer en casa = e _ _   o _ _

② rellenar una copa o vaso medio vacíos = t _ _   u _

③ brindar por alguien o algo = d _ _ _ _ _   t _

④ comer en casa = e _ _   i _

⑤ saber o tener mejor aspecto juntos = g _   t _ _ _ _ _ _ _ _

135

31.1 AFICIONES

Anastasia absolutely lives for skiing. She goes to the mountains whenever she can.

live for
tener pasión por algo, considerar algo lo más importante de tu vida

I recently got back into cycling. I hadn't done it since I was a teenager.

get back into
volver a hacer algo después de un tiempo sin hacerlo

It takes a while to get into horseback riding.

get into
interesarse por algo, empezar a disfrutar de una actividad

It's hard at first, but if you keep at it you'll start to love it.

keep at
continuar practicando una habilidad o actividad

Adi's painting skills are really coming along. He might become an artist one day.

come along
mejorar una habilidad o actividad

After she retired, Kim took up yoga. She does it for half an hour each morning.

take up
empezar a aprender una habilidad o actividad

31.2 DESCANSO

Nathan told his daughters to stop lazing about, and help to tidy the house.

laze about
descansar, no hacer nada

After the exam, the students went to the local park to wind down.

wind down
calmarse (tras un período de trabajo o agitación)

On my days off work, I like to sit around the garden doing nothing.

sit around
pasar tiempo sentado, sin hacer nada

I spend most Sundays lying around the house.

lie around
relajarse en el sofá o la cama

Ver también: come along **5**, **52**   get into **23**
get out of **17**   pick up **9**, **10**, **11**, **28**, **38**
take up **15**, **55**   throw away **28**   wind down **23**

Learning the piano isn't easy, but if you **stick at** it, you could become a great pianist.

stick at (UK)
continuar practicando una habilidad o actividad a pesar de las dificultades

While working in Seoul I tried to **pick up** some Korean by talking to local people.

pick up
aprender una habilidad de manera informal

If you want to be a great tennis player, it helps if you **start out** at a young age.

start out
empezar una afición o una profesión

Ken's currently **working toward** getting a black belt in judo.

work toward
invertir tiempo en algo con el objetivo de conseguir algo

Fabio could have been a great guitarist, but he **threw** it all **away** by never practicing.

throw away
desaprovechar un talento u oportunidad

I found running very hard when I started, but I **get** a lot of satisfaction **out of** it now.

get out of
disfrutar

Luiza spent the evening **curled up** on the couch reading a book.

curl up
estirarse o sentarse con los brazos y las piernas acurrucados

After a stressful day, I take a bath to help me **chill out**.

chill out
relajarse, dejar de estar enfadado o estresado

Aden needs to **loosen up**. Tell him to come and dance with us!

loosen up
relajarse, dejar la formalidad de lado

On Friday evenings, Josh likes to **kick back** and watch some television.

kick back
dejar de trabajar y relajarse (informal)

Aa 31.3 TACHA LAS PALABRAS INCORRECTAS DE CADA FRASE

It takes a while to get into / ~~behind~~ / ~~above~~ horseback riding.

1. Ken's currently working around / toward / for getting a black belt in judo.

2. Nathan told his daughters to stop lazing beside / about / along, and help to tidy the house.

3. After the exam, the students went to the local park to wind low / below / down.

4. I recently got back into / onto / for cycling. I hadn't done it since I was a teenager.

5. On Friday evenings, Josh likes to kick ahead / back / around and watch some television.

6. Anastasia absolutely lives by / on / for skiing. She goes to the mountains whenever she can.

Aa 31.4 CONECTA LAS IMÁGENES CON LAS FRASES CORRECTAS

I found running very hard when I started, but I get a lot of satisfaction out of it now.

1

While working in Seoul I tried to pick up some Korean by talking to local people.

2

Fabio could have been a great guitarist, but he threw it all away by never practicing.

3

Learning the piano isn't easy, but if you stick at it, you could become a great pianist.

4

Adi's painting skills are really coming along. He might become an artist one day.

31.5 ESCUCHA EL AUDIO Y CONECTA LAS IMÁGENES CON LOS PHRASAL VERBS CORRECTOS

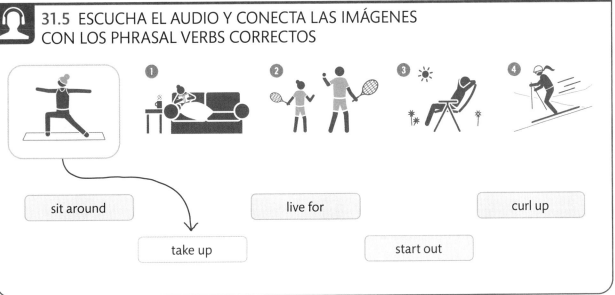

sit around

take up

live for

start out

curl up

Aa 31.6 VUELVE A ESCRIBIR LAS FRASES PONIENDO LAS PALABRAS EN SU ORDEN CORRECTO

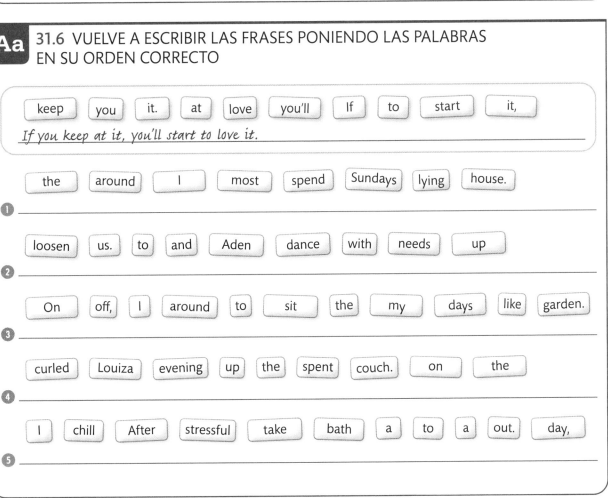

keep · you · it. · at · love · you'll · If · to · start · it,

If you keep at it, you'll start to love it.

the · around · I · most · spend · Sundays · lying · house.

1 _____

loosen · us. · to · and · Aden · dance · with · needs · up

2 _____

On · off, · I · around · to · sit · the · my · days · like · garden.

3 _____

curled · Louiza · evening · up · the · spent · couch. · on · the

4 _____

I · chill · After · stressful · take · bath · a · to · a · out. · day,

5 _____

32 Salud

32.1 SALUD

My son always bounces back **quickly whenever he gets ill.**

bounce back
recuperarse rápidamente o sin dificultad

The wound seems to be healing up **well. It will be better soon.**

heal up (UK)
(una herida) sanar por completo

Elaine's rash began to clear up **after she started using the cream.**

clear up
irse o mejorar

My brother's a nurse. He cares for **sick people at the local hospital.**

care for
cuidar

There's a bad cold going around **my office at the moment. Everyone is ill.**

go around
contagiar de persona a persona

Mona has an awful headache. She doesn't feel up to **working today.**

feel up to
sentirse bien

Paola's hay fever usually flares up **in the spring.**

flare up
aparecer o reaparecer de repente

It's taken me weeks to get over **this cold, but I finally feel better.**

get over
recuperarse, sentirse bien de nuevo

Danny's thumb swelled up **after he was stung by a wasp.**

swell up
(una hinchazón) crecer

After a few hours, the swelling had started to go down.

go down
(una hinchazón) disminuir

Ver también:
care for **3**   clear up **11**, **50**   get over **45**, **53**
go around **54**   go down **12**, **54**   pass on **38**

I think I'm coming down with the flu.
I have a headache and my nose
is running.

come down with
enfermar con

When Rachel came around after the
operation, her husband was
sitting at her bedside.

come around
recuperar la conciencia

I was very sad to hear that your
grandmother has passed away.

pass away
morir

My son passed on the virus
to his sisters.

pass on
contagiar a alguien

One of the musicians passed out during
the performance this evening.

pass out
*desmayarse, perder
la conciencia*

It was a very risky operation,
but Josh pulled through.

pull through
*sobrevivir a una enfermedad
grave u operación complicada*

Tina's leg muscles seized up after she
had completed the marathon.

seize up
ponerse rígido, moverse con dificultad

I've been ill for weeks, but I've finally
managed to shake it off.

shake off
recuperarse por completo

Ella's been throwing up all day. She must
be suffering from food poisoning.

throw up
vomitar

As the painkiller wore off, Shahid's
tooth began to ache again.

wear off
perder efectividad de forma gradual

32.2 CONECTA LAS DEFINICIONES CON LOS PHRASAL VERBS CORRECTOS

recuperarse rápidamente o sin dificultad	heal up
❶ sanar por completo	throw up
❷ vomitar	bounce back
❸ aparecer o reaparecer de repente	go around
❹ recuperar la conciencia	seize up
❺ ponerse rígido, moverse con dificultad	come around
❻ contagiar de persona a persona	flare up

32.3 TACHA LAS PALABRAS INCORRECTAS DE CADA FRASE

 It was a very risky operation, but Josh pulled under / over / through.

❶ Elaine's rash began to clear out / in / up after she started using the cream.

❷ I think I'm coming down with / for / to the flu.

❸ Ella's been throwing over / up / down all day.

❹ My son passed over / through / on the virus to his sisters.

❺ It's taken me weeks to get over / around / through this cold, but I finally feel better.

32.4 ESCUCHA EL AUDIO Y COMPLETA LAS FRASES QUE DESCRIBEN LAS IMÁGENES

One of the musicians ___*passed out*___ during the performance this evening.

3 Danny's thumb _____ after he was stung by a wasp.

1 Paola's hay fever usually _____ in the spring.

4 My brother's a nurse. He _____ sick people at the local hospital.

2 After a few hours, the swelling had started to _____ .

5 I was very sad to hear that your grandmother has _____ .

Aa ## 32.5 ESCRIBE EL PHRASAL VERB CORRECTO AL LADO DE SU DEFINICIÓN

ponerse rígido, moverse con dificultad	=	*seize up*
1 cuidar	=	_____
2 sentirse bien	=	_____
3 contagiar de persona a persona	=	_____
4 perder su efectividad de forma gradual	=	_____
5 sobrevivir a una enfermedad grave u operación complicada	=	_____

33 Deporte y ejercicio

33.1 DEPORTE

Clara was sent off the pitch after pushing over another player.

send off
expulsar del partido por no cumplir las normas

Angela knocked Kirsten out in the first round of the competition.

knock out (of)
derrotar a un equipo o jugador, eliminarlo de la competición

The crowd cheered Tony on as he approached the finish line.

cheer on
animar a alguien

Pete wanted to start playing baseball, so he signed up for his school team.

sign up (for)
unirse a un equipo, apuntarse a una actividad

My sister is a judo champion. She ranks among the best in the country.

rank among
estar entre

Five runners have gotten through to the final. Whoever wins this race gets the trophy.

get through (to)
llegar (a una fase de una competición)

33.2 EJERCICIO

After a big meal, Chris goes for a brisk walk to burn off the extra calories.

burn off
consumir energía (haciendo ejercicio)

For this yoga position, you have to stretch your arms out as far as you can.

stretch out
estirar

Playing tennis all afternoon with Gus has worn Charlie out.

wear out
cansar mucho

Jamal was completely wiped out after cycling up the mountain.

wipe out
agotar

Ver también:
aim at **34**   get through (to) **38**   keep from **51**   keep up (with) **20**   send off **38**
turn around **19**   warm up **11**   wear out **49**   work out **20**, **26**

rank watched Phillip play tennis. He was
izing up his opponent before
he next day's match.

ze up
*arse (en una persona o una situación)
decidir cómo actuar*

It looked like the Eagles were going to
lose the match, but they turned
it around at the last minute.

turn around
*hacer que una mala situación
mejore*

picked up my bow and aimed
nother arrow at the target.

im at
irigir algo hacia otra cosa

Sami invited me to join in a game of cricket.

join in
*participar en algo que ya
están haciendo otros*

My knee injury kept me from completing
he marathon this year.

eep from
vitar que alguien haga algo

I struggle to keep up with my brother.
He's much fitter than I am.

keep up (with)
moverse a la misma velocidad

🔊

After a long day in the office,
laying squash helps me
o work off all my stress.

ork off
*astar energía, deshacerse
e una emoción*

After finishing the race, Sandra warmed
down by stretching her legs.

warm down
*estirar y relajar el cuerpo
tras el ejercicio*

efore playing a game of soccer, I always
varm up by jogging slowly.

arm up
reparar el cuerpo para el ejercicio

Leo works out at his local gym
every morning.

work out
hacer ejercicio

🔊

Aa 33.3 COMPLETA LOS ESPACIOS CON LAS PALABRAS DEL RECUADRO PARA CREAR PHRASAL VERBS

After a big meal, Chris goes for a brisk walk to [burn *off*] the extra calories.

1 After finishing the race, Sandra [warmed] by stretching her legs.

2 Jamal was completely [wiped] after cycling up the mountain.

3 Clara was [sent] the pitch after pushing over another player.

4 Five runners have [gotten] to the final. Whoever wins this race will win the trophy.

5 My sister is a judo champion. She [ranks] the best in the country.

6 I struggle to [keep] with my brother. He's much fitter than I am.

[out   among   ~~off~~   through   up   down   off]

Aa 33.4 MARCA LAS FRASES CORRECTAS

Playing tennis all afternoon with Gus has worn Charlie out. ☑
Playing tennis all afternoon with Gus has worn Charlie off. ☐

1 Before playing a game of soccer, I always warm down by jogging slowly. ☐
Before playing a game of soccer, I always warm up by jogging slowly. ☐

2 For this yoga position, you have to stretch your arms out as far as you can. ☐
For this yoga position, you have to stretch your arms in as far as you can. ☐

3 Pete wanted to start playing baseball, so he signed on for his school team. ☐
Pete wanted to start playing baseball, so he signed up for his school team. ☐

4 Angela knocked Kirsten out in the first round of the competition. ☐
Angela knocked Kirsten down in the first round of the competition. ☐

5 My knee injury kept me through completing the marathon this year. ☐
My knee injury kept me from completing the marathon this year. ☐

33.5 ESCUCHA EL AUDIO Y ESCRIBE LAS FRASES BAJO LAS IMÁGENES

Sami invited me to join in a game of cricket.

1 _____

_____

2 _____

_____

3 _____

_____

4 _____

_____

5 _____

_____

Aa 33.6 ESCRIBE EL PHRASAL VERB CORRECTO AL LADO DE SU DEFINICIÓN

dirigir algo hacia otra cosa	=	*aim at*
1 moverse a la misma velocidad	=	_____
2 preparar el cuerpo para el ejercicio	=	_____
3 fijarse (en una persona o situación) y decidir cómo actuar	=	_____
4 hacer que una mala situación mejore	=	_____
5 consumir energía (haciendo ejercicio)	=	_____
6 animar a alguien	=	_____
7 gastar energía, deshacerse de una emoción	=	_____

34 Artes

Ver también:
aim at 33

34.1 CREATIVIDAD

Sami and Shahid made the cardboard box into a robot.

make into
convertir algo en otra cosa

The architects have mocked up a model of the new museum.

mock up
hacer una maqueta de algo

Greg and Chloe colored in pictures of dinosaurs after their trip to the museum.

color in
usar lápices de colores o rotuladores para dar color a un dibujo

34.2 MEDIOS DE COMUNICACIÓN

The new music channel is aimed at people who like jazz.

aim at
estar pensado para o ir dirigido a

This new TV show feeds on people's curiosity about aliens.

feed on
aprovecharse de

I tune into my favorite radio show every Sunday morning.

tune into
mirar un programa en la televisión o escuchar una emisora en la radio

34.3 MÚSICA

At the start of the horror movie, scary music started to fade in.

fade in
aumentar el volumen gradualmente

As the music died away, the presenter stepped onto the stage.

die away
disminuir el volumen antes de acabar

The noise from the parade faded away as it moved away from us.

fade away
disminuir el volumen gradualmente

My new headphones help me concentrate by filtering out background noise.

filter out
retirar o bloquear algo

Aa 34.4 COMPLETA LOS ESPACIOS CON LOS PHRASAL VERBS DEL RECUADRO

As the music ___*died away*___ , the presenter stepped onto the stage.

1. The new music channel is _____ people who like jazz.

2. At the start of the horror movie, scary music started to _____ .

3. My new headphones help me concentrate by _____ background noise.

4. This new TV show _____ people's curiosity about aliens.

5. The noise from the parade _____ as it moved away from us.

6. I _____ my favorite radio show every Sunday morning.

feeds on   fade in   ~~died away~~   tune into   filtering out   aimed at   faded away

34.5 ESCUCHA EL AUDIO Y ESCRIBE LAS FRASES BAJO LAS IMÁGENES

Sami and Shahid made the cardboard box into a robot.

1. _____

2. _____

3. _____

4. _____

5. _____

35 Viajes

Ver también: arrive at **47** bring back **16** check out **10**, **50** end up **17**
get around **50**, **53** get away **13** get back (from) **1** go back **16**, **54**
go off **3**, **8**, **27**, **30** put up **28** set off **46**, **53** set out **23**, **53**

35.1 VIAJES

When Krishna arrived at the villa, the party had already begun.

arrive at
llegar al destino

During his vacation in Rome, Anton hired a moped to get around the city.

get around
ir de un lugar a otro

When they arrived at the hotel, Julia and John went to reception to check in.

check in(to)
registrar la llegada a un hotel o aeropuerto

Julia and John checked out of the hotel and went to the airport.

check out (of)
abandonar el hotel tras abonar la cuenta

On your way to London you'll pass by Cambridge, a beautiful university city.

pass by
pasar por un sitio (de camino hacia otro sitio)

Dan and I went to Paris for our honeymoon. We went back last month for our 25th wedding anniversary.

go back
volver a visitar

By the time we got back from our cycle ride, it was already getting dark.

get back from
volver de

We were supposed to hike to the mountain, but we ended up by the lake.

end up
llegar a algún sitio sin querer

Marimar and I went off to Miami recently.

go off (to)
irse de viaje o vacaciones

It was great to get away for a few days!

get away
ir a algún sitio para desconectar o relajarse

Hi Paula,
We're having a great time in Cyprus. Our hotel overlooks the sea. We soak up the atmosphere each morning as we have our coffee. We're packing in lots of sightseeing. We saw some ruins and a vineyard today. We're heading for Athens today. We can't wait! We'll bring you back some local olives. They're delicious!
See you soon!
Ted and Sandy

Our hotel overlooks the sea. We soak up the atmosphere each morning as we have our coffee.

soak up
mirar y escuchar, disfrutar

We're packing in lots of sightseeing during our vacation. We saw some ruins and a vineyard today.

pack in
hacer mucho de algo

We've been in Cyprus for a few days, but we're heading for Athens today.

head for
ir hacia un destino concreto

We brought you back some local olives. They're delicious!

bring back
volver con

Whenever we set out on a hike, we always take waterproofs, a compass, and a map.

set out (on)
empezar un viaje

We set off for Chicago at dawn when there would be less traffic on the roads.

set off (for)
empezar un viaje

On our way to Barcelona, we stopped over in a lovely hotel for the night.

stop over
pasar la noche en algún sitio de camino hacia otro sitio

We managed to put the tent up even though it was raining heavily.

put up
montar, levantar

35.2 ESCUCHA EL AUDIO Y MARCA LOS PHRASAL VERBS QUE APARECEN

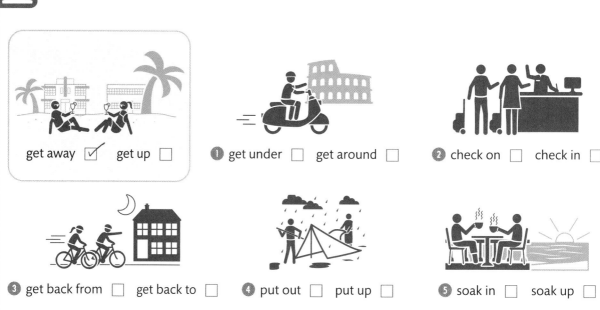

get away ☑   get up ☐

1 get under ☐   get around ☐

2 check on ☐   check in ☐

3 get back from ☐   get back to ☐

4 put out ☐   put up ☐

5 soak in ☐   soak up ☐

Aa 35.3 VUELVE A ESCRIBIR LAS FRASES PONIENDO LAS PALABRAS EN SU ORDEN CORRECTO

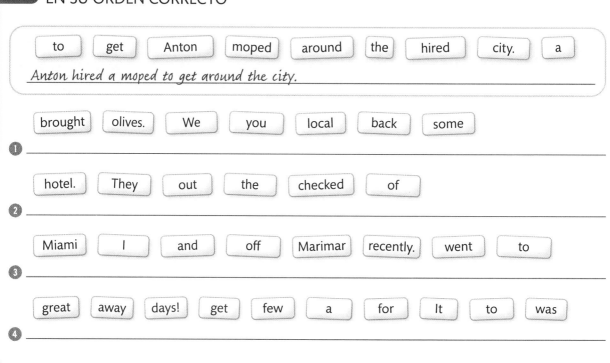

| to | get | Anton | moped | around | the | hired | city. | a |

Anton hired a moped to get around the city.

| brought | olives. | We | you | local | back | some |

1 _____

| hotel. | They | out | the | checked | of |

2 _____

| Miami | I | and | off | Marimar | recently. | went | to |

3 _____

| great | away | days! | get | few | a | for | It | to | was |

4 _____

35.4 CONECTA LOS PRINCIPIOS DE LAS FRASES CON LOS FINALES CORRECTOS

During his vacation in Rome,	we stopped over in a hotel for the night.
1 On our way to Barcelona,	Julia went to the reception to check in.
2 Whenever we set out on a hike,	Anton hired a moped to get around the city.
3 We set off for Chicago at dawn	even though it was raining heavily.
4 When she arrived at the hotel,	we always take a compass and a map.
5 We managed to put the tent up	when there would be less traffic.

35.5 COMPLETA LOS ESPACIOS CON LOS PHRASAL VERBS DEL RECUADRO

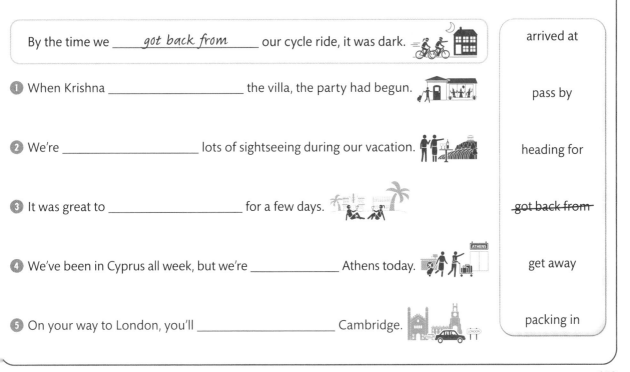

By the time we _____got back from_____ our cycle ride, it was dark.

arrived at

1 When Krishna _____ the villa, the party had begun.

pass by

2 We're _____ lots of sightseeing during our vacation.

heading for

3 It was great to _____ for a few days.

~~got back from~~

4 We've been in Cyprus all week, but we're _____ Athens today.

get away

5 On your way to London, you'll _____ Cambridge.

packing in

36.1 CONVERSACIONES

Ben's not keen on buying a new car. I'm trying to talk him round.

talk round (UK)
conseguir convencer a alguien

Kirsty talked the workers through the new software system.

talk through
explicar cómo funciona algo

Marco is always talking at people. He never gives them a chance to speak.

talk at
hablar a alguien y no dejar que conteste

My kids talked me into getting a puppy. They've promised to take care of it.

talk into
convencer a alguien para que haga algo

Shona wanted to dye her hair green, but her sister talked her out of it.

talk out of
convencer a alguien para que no haga algo

Every time Rita tries to say something, Greg talks over her.

talk over
hablar alto mientras alguien más está hablando

Uncle Toby still talks down to me like I'm a child, even though I'm 25.

talk down to
hablar con condescendencia

While Julia was explaining her idea, Rupert cut in to tell her she was wrong.

cut in
interrumpir

We were chatting about movies when Tina launched into a speech about her favorite actors.

launch into
empezar de repente a hablar con entusiasmo sobre algo

Simone spent the whole of lunch mouthing off about how much she hates her new boss.

mouth off
hablar de manera negativa sobre algo o alguien (informal)

Ver también:
blurt out **51**   come up **16, 50, 52**
talk over **22**

> Shut up and listen to me for once!

> I think you should tone down your language.

shut up
hacer callar (irrespetuoso)

tone down
hablar de forma menos agresiva

I couldn't hear Louise at all. The man next to us was completely **drowning her out.**

drown out
hablar más alto que otra persona

Lauren **comes out with** the funniest things. Today she told me she wants to live on the Moon.

come out with
decir algo sorprendente

Diana is always **rambling on** about how things were better when she was a child.

ramble on
hablar durante mucho tiempo de algo (de una manera pesada o incoherente)

The lecturer **droned on** for what felt like hours. We were half asleep by the end.

drone on
hablar durante mucho tiempo de una manera muy aburrida

Craig was trying to tell a joke, but **tailed off** as he realized that no one was listening.

tail off
dejar de hablar gradualmente

After the concert, I **struck up** a conversation with one of the guitarists.

strike up
empezar una conversación

When soccer **came up in** conversation, Bill and I realized we support the same team.

come up (in)
aparecer en una conversación, en general de manera inesperada

Andy **blurted out** the name of the winner. It was supposed to be a secret.

blurt out
decir algo sin pensarlo antes

Every time Rita tries to say something,

1. Kirsty talked the workers
2. Shona wanted to dye her hair purple,
3. Diana is always rambling on about
4. Uncle Toby still talks down to me
5. Shut up
6. My kids talked me into

through the new software system.

getting a puppy.

Greg talks over her.

and listen to me for once!

how things were better when she was a child.

like I'm a child, even though I'm 25.

but her sister talked her out of it.

Aa **36.3** CONECTA LOS VERBOS CON LAS PARTÍCULAS CORRECTAS PARA CONSTRUIR PHRASAL VERBS

strike — down

1. drown / into
2. mouth → up
3. ramble / out
4. tone / on
5. talk / through
6. launch / off

36.4 ESCUCHA EL AUDIO Y LUEGO NUMERA LAS IMÁGENES EN EL ORDEN EN QUE APARECEN

A ☐   B 1

C ☐   D ☐

E ☐   F ☐

36.5 COMPLETA LOS ESPACIOS CON LOS PHRASAL VERBS DEL RECUADRO

Uncle Toby still _talks down to_ me like I'm a child, even though I'm 25.

droned on

struck up

~~talks down to~~

talking at

tone down

blurted out

① I think you should _____ your language.

② Andy _____ the name of the winner by mistake.

③ The lecturer _____ for what felt like hours.

④ Marco is always _____ people and not letting them speak.

⑤ After the concert, I _____ a conversation with the guitarist.

36.6 VUELVE A ESCRIBIR LAS FRASES CORRIGIENDO LOS ERRORES

Lauren **goes out with** the funniest things. Today she told me she wants to live on the Moon.
Lauren comes out with the funniest things. Today she told me she wants to live on the Moon.

① Ben's not keen on buying a new car. I'm trying to **talk** him **straight**.

_____

② When soccer **came down in** conversation, Bill and I realized we support the same team.

_____

③ Craig was trying to tell a joke, but **tailed up** as he realized that no one was listening.

_____

④ While Julia was explaining her idea, Rupert **chopped in** to tell her she was wrong.

_____

⑤ Simone spent the whole of lunch **teething off** about how much she hates her new boss.

_____

37 Leer y escribir

37.1 ESCRIBIR

Before you can use the gym, you need to fill in this form.

fill in
rellenar un formulario

Miguel scribbled down **a note to his housemate to say that he was going out for the evening.**

scribble down
leer algo rápido o en diagonal

Ted always writes out **his essays instead of typing them.**

write out
escribir algo a mano completamente

Celia read through her notes from today's lecture and typed **them** up.

type up
teclear algo a partir de apuntes

The journalist jotted down **the details as Dan described his role in the new movie.**

jot down
tomar apuntes rápidamente

37.2 LEER

I've only dipped into **Nia's new novel, but it's fantastic so far.**

dip into
leer un breve fragmento de un libro o texto

It stands for **Unidentified Flying Object.**

What does UFO mean?

stand for
ser la abreviatura de

We pored over **the old document looking for clues.**

pore over
leer con mucha atención

Adventures in the Wilderness should make for **interesting reading!**

make for
resultar en

Ver también:
cut out **9**   fill in **40**   make for **52**

> Your essay's too long, Marcel. You need to cut it down a bit.

> Okay. I'll try to cut out 500 words.

cut down
reducir en tamaño

cut out
eliminar fragmentos de un texto

When I write a restaurant review I usually write down a few thoughts while I'm eating.

write down
registrar información escribiéndola

I write up my review at home later that evening.

write up
redactar algo a partir de apuntes

When completing the form, Damian wrote in his age.

write in
introducir información escribiéndola

Paco read the book and noted down the most important points.

note down
tomar apuntes

Alexandra flicked through a magazine while she waited to get her hair cut.

flick through
echar una ojeada rápida a un libro o revista

Max read through the full report before giving his opinion.

read through
leer algo de principio a final

As the judge read out the names of the winners, Pablo waited hopefully.

read out
leer en voz alta (para que lo oigan los demás)

Fatima read up on ancient Greece before her history exam.

read up on
investigar o revisar un tema

Aa 37.3 CONECTA LOS PHRASAL VERBS CON LAS DEFINICIONES CORRECTAS

read out	escribir algo rápido o en borrador
① note down	leer con mucha atención
② cut down	leer en voz alta (para que lo oigan los demás)
③ write up	rellenar un formulario
④ scribble down	redactar algo a partir de apuntes
⑤ stand for	reducir en tamaño
⑥ pore over	ser la abreviatura de
⑦ fill in	tomar apuntes

Aa 37.4 MARCA LAS FRASES CORRECTAS

I've only dipped into Nia's new novel, but it's fantastic so far. ☑

I've only dipped over Nia's new novel, but it's fantastic so far. ☐

① Before you can use the gym, you need to fill in this form. ☐

Before you can use the gym, you need to fill on this form. ☐

② As the judge read in the names of the winners, Pablo waited hopefully. ☐

As the judge read out the names of the winners, Pablo waited hopefully. ☐

③ When completing the form, Damian wrote on his age. ☐

When completing the form, Damian wrote in his age. ☐

④ Alexandra flicked through a magazine while she waited to get her hair cut. ☐

Alexandra flicked above a magazine while she waited to get her hair cut. ☐

37.5 MIRA LAS IMÁGENES Y COMPLETA LAS FRASES CON PHRASAL VERBS
DEL RECUADRO

Miguel _scribbled down_ a note to his
housemate to say that he was going out.

③ "UFO" _____ Unidentified
Flying Object.

① Max _____ the full report before
giving his opinion.

④ The journalist _____ the details
as Dan described his role in the new movie.

② Ted always _____ his essays
instead of typing them.

⑤ Fatima _____ on ancient Greece
before her history exam.

stands for	~~scribbled down~~	read up	writes out	jotted down	read through

---

37.6 COMPLETA LOS ESPACIOS CON LAS PALABRAS DEL RECUADRO
PARA CREAR PHRASAL VERBS

When I write a restaurant review, I usually [write _down_] a few thoughts while I'm eating.

① I'll try to [cut _____] 500 words from my essay if it is too long.

② *Adventures in the Wilderness* should [make _____] interesting reading!

③ Paco read the book and [noted _____] the most important points.

④ We [pored _____] the old document looking for clues.

for	out	~~down~~	over	down

38 Seguir en contacto

Ver también: break up **3**, **15**, **21**, **29**   get through (to) **33**   hang up **6**   pass on **32**   pick up **9**, **10**, **11**, **28**, **31**   put through **55**   send off **33**

38.1 POR TELÉFONO

I had to call Megan six times before she finally picked up the phone.

pick up
contestar una llamada telefónica

Hi Laura, sorry I'm cooking at the moment. Can I call you back in 10 minutes?

call back
devolver una llamada, llamar a alguien que intentó hablar contigo antes

Anna works from home on Tuesdays, so she will dial into the meeting.

dial in(to)
unirse a una llamada múltiple

After chatting for over an hour, Simon and I said goodbye and hung up.

hang up
acabar una llamada telefónica (a menudo de repente)

Could you please speak up? I can't hear you very well!

speak up
hablar más alto

I've called Olly a few times this evening, but I can't get through.

get through (to)
contactar con alguien por teléfono

Sorry, I can't hear you very well, I'm afraid. You keep breaking up.

break up
tener problemas de sonido (por mala señal)

I phoned around to ask if any of my friends wanted to go to the beach with me.

phone around
llamar a varias personas

Could I speak to Mr. Yamamoto, please?

Certainly. I'll put you through now, madam.

put through (to)
conectar a alguien con la persona con la que desea hablar

38.2 DEJAR UN MENSAJE

Dave passed on a message telling me that Rob had called.

pass on
darle a alguien un mensaje que te han dejado a ti

Hi Ulrika,

Rob called and asked me to pass on a message. He wants to follow up on your chat about the new logo last week. Can you get back to him as soon as you can?

Dave

Rob wants to follow up on the conversation we had about the new logo.

follow up on
encontrar más información, hacer algo en respuesta a algo

He asked me to get back to him as soon as possible.

get back (to)
responder a una llamada o mensaje de alguien que te llamó o escribió antes

---

38.3 ENVIAR Y RESPONDER

I love receiving letters from my dad. I always write back immediately.

write back
responder por carta o correo electrónico

Claudia sent wedding invitations out to all her friends and family.

send out (to)
enviar a un grupo de personas

I sent Paul a text asking him where he was. He texted back saying he was on the train.

text back
responder por mensaje de texto

Chris emailed me a week ago, but I only just remembered to email him back.

email back
responder por correo electrónico

Our company is trying to reach out to new customers by offering discounts.

reach out (to)
ponerse en contacto

Murat completed all the forms and sent them off to the passport office.

send off (to)
enviar algo por carta o correo electrónico

38.4 TACHA LAS PALABRAS INCORRECTAS DE CADA FRASE

I had to call Megan six times before she finally picked ~~out~~ / ~~over~~ / up the phone.

① Rob wants to chase / follow / catch up on the conversation we had about the new logo.

② Claudia sent wedding invitations up / off / out to all her friends and family.

③ Dave passed up / off / on a message telling me that Rob had called.

④ Sorry, I can't hear you very well, I'm afraid. You keep crumbling / breaking / tearing up.

⑤ I've called Olly a few times this evening, but I can't get among / into / through.

⑥ Could you please speak down / on / up ? I can't hear you very well!

Aa 38.5 CONECTA LAS IMÁGENES CON LAS FRASES CORRECTAS

Murat completed all the forms and sent them off to the passport office.

①

I sent Paul a text asking him where he was. He texted back saying he was on the train.

②

Claudia sent wedding invitations out to all her friends and family.

③

Chris emailed me a week ago, but I only just remembered to email him back.

④

I love receiving letters from my dad. I always write back immediately.

38.6 ESCUCHA EL AUDIO Y CONECTA LAS IMÁGENES CON LOS PHRASAL VERBS CORRECTOS

pick up

hang up

speak up

put through

call back

Aa 38.7 COMPLETA LOS ESPACIOS PONIENDO LAS PALABRAS EN SU ORDEN CORRECTO

back   get   to

He asked me to ___*get*___ ___*back*___ ___*to*___ him as soon as possible.

the   into   dial

1 Anna works from home on Tuesdays, so she will _____ _____ _____ meeting.

through   you   put

2 I'll _____ _____ _____ to Mr. Yamamoto now, madam.

reach   to   out

3 Our company is trying to _____ _____ _____ new customers by offering discounts.

up   hung   and

4 After chatting for over an hour, Simon and I said goodbye _____ _____ _____ .

back   you   call

5 Hi Laura, sorry I'm cooking at the moment, can I _____ _____ _____ in 10 minutes?

39 Pensamientos e ideas

Ver también: come across **1**, **52**
think through **50**
throw out **17**

39.1 IDEAS

They **bombarded** us with **too much information during the training course.**

bombard with
*hacer demasiadas preguntas,
dar demasiada información*

Gill and the design team are **bouncing ideas off** each other before the show next week.

bounce off
*intercambiar ideas creativas para
ver cómo responden los demás*

The president's speech **touched on** the economy, healthcare, and education.

touch on
*comentar brevemente algo
en una charla o texto*

I wrote a proposal for more environmentally friendly policies and **put** it **to** the directors.

put to
*sugerir algo para que otros
elijan aceptarlo o no*

When my husband suggested buying a new kitchen, I **ran with** it.

run with
hacer lo que alguien sugiere

When I told my friends I was starting my own business, they all **got behind** the idea.

get behind
ofrecer apoyo a alguien

The creative manager asked her team to **throw out** as many ideas as they could.

throw out
sugerir muchas ideas espontáneas

We have **ruled out** three of the candidates. It's a choice between Danny and Carmen.

rule out
*descartar algo o a alguien
antes de tomar una decisión*

Ted has **come up with** some good ideas for a new logo.

come up with
tener una idea, sugerencia o plan

He decided to **put forward** the version with the star.

put forward
ofrecer una opinión, idea o sugerencia

39.2 DARSE CUENTA

The artist's feelings of anger come across very strongly in this painting.

come across
transmitirse

Experts have attributed this painting to Joan Miró because of the distinctive style.

attribute to
creer que alguien concreto dijo o creó algo

It finally dawned on me that Claude was the killer.

dawn on
quedarle claro algo a alguien

It had never occurred to me that such a charming character could commit such a terrible crime.

occur to
venir de repente algo a la cabeza

39.3 PENSAMIENTOS

While writing her memoir, Rebecca reflected on her childhood.

reflect on
pensar en algo de manera diligente

Before deciding whether or not to move to Canada, we need to think it through.

think through
reflexionar sobre las ventajas y desventajas de algo

Selma is very creative. She thinks up lots of wonderful dishes.

think up
pensar un nuevo plan o idea

There's a lot to think about when buying a house, but it often boils down to money.

boil down to
ser el principal motivo

I asked Zoya if she'd like to work for us. She's thinking it over, and will let us know tomorrow.

think over
reflexionar mucho sobre un plan o idea antes de tomar una decisión

The teacher asked us all to think of a famous person from history and write a story about them.

think of
crearse una imagen mental de algo o alguien

39.4 ESCUCHA EL AUDIO Y LUEGO NUMERA LAS IMÁGENES EN EL ORDEN EN QUE APARECEN

A ☐

B 1

C ☐

D ☐

E ☐

F ☐

G ☐

H ☐

Aa 39.5 CONECTA LAS FRASES QUE SIGNIFICAN LO MISMO

The president's speech touched on the economy, healthcare, and education.

When I told my friends I was starting my own business, they all offered support.

① When my husband suggested buying a new kitchen, I ran with it.

The president's speech briefly mentioned the economy, healthcare, and education.

② When I told my friends I was starting my own business, they all got behind the idea.

Experts believe that Joan Miró created this painting because of the distinctive style.

③ They bombarded us with too much information during the training course.

When my husband suggested buying a new kitchen, I did what he suggested.

④ Experts have attributed this painting to Joan Miró because of the distinctive style.

The artist's feelings of anger are communicated strongly in this painting.

⑤ The artist's feelings of anger come across strongly in this painting.

They gave us too much information during the training course.

Aa 39.6 ESCRIBE LOS PHRASAL VERBS DEL RECUADRO EN LOS GRUPOS CORRECTOS

SEPARABLES

_____

_____

_____

_____

_____

INSEPARABLES

_____ *run with* _____

_____

_____

_____

_____

come across   bounce off   come up with   put to   get behind   think through

~~run with~~   bombard with   touch on   think over

Aa 39.7 MIRA LAS IMÁGENES Y COMPLETA LAS FRASES CON PHRASAL VERBS

While writing her memoir, Rebecca _____*reflected on*_____ her childhood.

1 The creative manager asked her team to _____ as many ideas as they could.

2 It finally _____ me that Claude was the killer.

3 We have _____ three of the candidates. It's a choice between Danny and Carmen.

4 Ted has _____ some good ideas for a new logo.

5 Selma is very creative. She _____ lots of wonderful dishes.

Ver también:
fill in 37

40.1 EXPLICAR COSAS

The politician alluded to housing in his speech, but mostly spoke about transportation.

allude to
mencionar algo de forma indirecta

How many times do I have to spell it out to you? You're not allowed to use your phone in class.

spell out
explicar algo de forma muy clara (normalmente con ira o frustración)

During her speech, the senator kept coming back to her financial policies.

come back to
volver a un tema

The interviewer asked me to expand on my experience of working with animals.

expand on
aportar más detalles sobre algo

I asked the professor if he could go back over some of the points from the lecture.

go back over
volver a explicar los detalles de algo

Pete couldn't remember the French word for "swimming," so he acted it out.

act out
explicar o enseñar algo actuando o recreándolo

Yuri managed to put his ideas across very well during the debate.

put across
lograr explicar una idea o expresar un sentimiento

My friend pointed out some of the mistakes I'd made in my code.

point out
ayudar a alguien a darse cuenta de algo

Becky asked Sarah to fill her in on the latest gossip from the office.

fill (someone) in (on)
aportar la información más reciente o importante sobre algo

Gio didn't know anything about computers, so he asked the salesperson to dumb it down for him.

dumb down
explicar algo de manera más fácil

40.2 ESCUCHA EL AUDIO Y MARCA LOS PHRASAL VERBS QUE APARECEN

spell out ☑
allude to ☐

❶ expand on ☐
point out ☐

❷ act out ☐
dumb down ☐

❸ come back to ☐
expand on ☐

❹ fill in on ☐
point out ☐

❺ put across ☐
go back over ☐

Aa ## 40.3 ESCRIBE EL PHRASAL VERB CORRECTO AL LADO DE SU DEFINICIÓN, COMPLETANDO LAS LETRAS QUE FALTAN

aportar más detalles sobre algo	=	e x p a n d o n

❶ lograr explicar una idea o expresar un sentimiento = p _ _   a _ _ _ _ _ _

❷ explicar algo de manera más fácil = d _ _ _   d _ _ _ _

❸ ayudar a alguien a darse cuenta de algo = p _ _ _ _   o _ _

❹ volver a un tema = c _ _ _   b _ _ _   t _

❺ mencionar algo de forma indirecta = a _ _ _ _ _ _   t _

❻ volver a explicar los detalles de algo = g _   b _ _ _   o _ _ _

41 Verdades y mentiras

41.1 VERDADES

I never caught on that Dad's company was in such debt.

catch on
darse cuenta de algo

When it came out that he was bankrupt, I was shocked!

come out
conocerse

Conan finally owned up to breaking the window. He'd been denying it all morning.

own up (to)
admitir que algo fue culpa tuya

I have to level with you, Anu. The cake looks lovely, but it tastes terrible.

level with
contarle la verdad a alguien

41.2 MENTIRAS

We fell for the salesman's talk. The car we bought broke down after a few days.

fall for
creerse algo que no era verdad

Pio's always making up excuses for handing in his homework late. Today, he claimed his school bag had been stolen.

make up
inventarse una historia para explicar algo

Tyler has been promising to pay me back for months, but he's just stringing me along.

string along
dar falsas esperanzas a alguien o hacer que se crea algo que es falso

Alice accused me of messing her around when I canceled our date for a third time.

mess around
tratar mal a alguien engañándole o cambiando de planes habitualmente

After eating all the cake, John tried to cover it up by claiming the dog had eaten it.

cover up
ocultar la verdad a otras personas

Larry's claim that he was at home on the night of the crime didn't add up.

add up
tener sentido, ser una explicación lógica

Ver también:
add up **14**, **25**   come out **5**, **12**   cover up **6**   fall for **3**   make out **52**
make up **44**, **52**   mess around **21**   put on **6**, **27**, **55**

It's really hard to suss the new neighbors out. They don't say anything about themselves.

suss out (UK)
entender lo que quiere alguien, o qué tipo de persona es

I've been trying to find out from Nisha who Sammy's dating.

find out
descubrir información

Gary was always exaggerating about how rich he was, but Safiya could see through his lies.

see through
ser consciente de que algo no es verdad

I think she knows more than she's letting on.

let on
admitir o revelar algo

Amrit promised his mother he'd stay home and study, but she caught him out when she heard him come home late.

catch out
descubrir que alguien está mintiendo

Josie tried to explain away the damage to my car by saying it was just a small scratch.

explain away
intentar convencer a alguien de que un problema no es importante o no es culpa tuya

The CEO has been playing down the company's financial problems.

play down
hacer que un problema parezca trivial

Mario glossed over the bad result, claiming the team would soon be back on form.

gloss over
intentar que una mala noticia o un error parezca trivial

Kirstie's been making out that everything's okay, but I know she's stressed about her interview.

make out
fingir

It looked as if Aaron had been injured, but I knew he was putting it on.

put on
fingir

173

Aa 41.3 CONECTA LAS DEFINICIONES CON LOS PHRASAL VERBS CORRECTOS

Definición		Phrasal verb
descubrir que alguien está mintiendo	→	see through
① ser consciente de que algo no es verdad		level with
② intentar que una mala noticia o un error parezca trivial	→	catch out
③ ocultar la verdad a otras personas		add up
④ tener sentido, ser una explicación lógica		cover up
⑤ creerse algo que no era verdad		gloss over
⑥ inventarse una historia para explicar algo		fall for
⑦ contarle la verdad a alguien		make up

41.4 ESCUCHA EL AUDIO Y MARCA LOS PHRASAL VERBS QUE APARECEN

suss out	✓	explain away	☐	see through	☐
① play down	☐	make up	☐	make out	☐
② cover up	☐	come out	☐	level with	☐
③ let on	☐	find out	☐	mess around	☐
④ gloss over	☐	string along	☐	add up	☐
⑤ put on	☐	catch out	☐	own up	☐
⑥ catch on	☐	explain away	☐	fall for	☐

41.5 MIRA LAS IMÁGENES Y COMPLETA LAS FRASES CON PHRASAL VERBS DEL RECUADRO

I never _____*caught on*_____ that Dad's company was in such debt.

④ Conan finally _____ to breaking the window. He'd been denying it all morning.

① I think she knows more than she's _____ .

⑤ The CEO has been _____ the company's financial problems.

② We _____ the salesman's talk. The car we bought broke down after a few days.

⑥ I've been trying to _____ from Nisha who Sammy's dating.

③ When it _____ that he was bankrupt, I was shocked!

⑦ Josie tried to _____ the damage to my car by saying it was just a small scratch.

fell for	explain away	find out	letting on	owned up
	came out	~~caught on~~		playing down

42 Animar

42.1 ANIMAR Y CONVENCER

The thought of winning first prize spurred Farukh on.

spur on
animar a alguien, inspirar a alguien para que haga algo

Helen has put me onto this great new hair salon. I'm going to check it out.

put onto
explicarle a alguien algo que puede serle útil

When Zoe asked her daughter why she'd stolen the cookies, she said her elder brother had put her up to it.

put up to
animar a alguien a hacer algo que está mal

Lisa's speech in favor of a new nature reserve has brought many people around to the idea.

bring around
convencer a alguien para que apoye tu idea

Kendra was very nervous, but was happy to see her friends rooting for her.

root for
mostrar apoyo por alguien

My son was upset, so I bought him an ice cream to buck him up.

buck up
hacer que alguien sea más feliz

Marcus's friends egged him on as he climbed the tree.

egg on
animar a alguien a hacer algo (a menudo alguna travesura)

The crowd urged Mona on as she approached the end of the tightrope.

urge on
animar a alguien para que haga algo

Rahul was skeptical about electric cars until the salesman reasoned with him.

reason with
dar argumentos lógicos para intentar que alguien cambie de opinión

He eventually won him over by explaining how eco-friendly they are.

win over
conseguir convencer a alguien para que apoye tu idea

Aa 42.2 MARCA LAS FRASES CORRECTAS

The thought of winning first prize spurred Farukh on.	☑
The thought of winning first prize spurred Farukh off.	☐

1 Helen has put me onto this great new hair salon. I'm going to check it out. ☐
Helen has taken me onto this great new hair salon. I'm going to check it out. ☐

2 Lisa's speech in favor of a new nature reserve has brought many people around to the idea. ☐
Lisa's speech in favor of a new nature reserve has brought many people about to the idea. ☐

3 Kendra was very nervous, but was happy to see her friends planting for her. ☐
Kendra was very nervous, but was happy to see her friends rooting for her. ☐

4 Zoe's daughter said her elder brother had put her up to stealing the cookies. ☐
Zoe's daughter said her elder brother had put her onto stealing the cookies. ☐

42.3 ESCUCHA EL AUDIO Y COMPLETA LAS FRASES QUE DESCRIBEN LAS IMÁGENES

Marcus's friends __egged__ him ___on___ as he climbed the tree.

1 Kendra was very nervous, but was happy to see her friends _____ her.

2 Rahul was skeptical about electric cars until the salesman _____ him.

3 The crowd _____ Mona _____ as she approached the end of the tightrope.

4 He eventually _____ him _____ by explaining how eco-friendly they are.

5 My son was upset, so I bought him an ice cream to _____ him _____ .

43 Acuerdos y desacuerdos

43.1 ACUERDOS Y DESACUERDOS

Everyone agrees with John that Sian should get the job.

agree with
tener la misma opinión que alguien

Martin and Simon disagreed with each other about what color to paint the kitchen.

disagree with
creer que algo está mal o que alguien no tiene razón

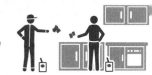

I want to go on an expensive vacation this year. I'm trying to persuade my husband to go along with the idea.

go along with
aceptar hacer algo a regañadientes

My aunt frowns on people wearing shoes indoors. She makes her friends take them off when they visit.

frown on
desaprobar algo

I can always count on my sister to comfort me when I'm upset.

count on
confiar en alguien

Laura objected to Ankita's proposals for the new restaurant.

object to
oponerse a algo

During the debate, the politician hit out at her opponents.

hit out at
criticar mucho a alguien

Danny pulled Roberta up on her attitude towards the environment.

pull up on (UK)
criticar a alguien por algo concreto

Our local representative has come out against the plans for a new housing development.

come out against
revelar en público tu oposición a algo

Whenever there's a disagreement at work, Paulina always sides with our boss. It's so irritating!

side with
apoyar a alguien en una discusión

Ver también:
push back **16**

Carla stood up to **the bullies. She told them to stop being mean to her brother.**

stand up to
*defender a alguien o a ti mismo
frente a alguien más*

The workers at the factory are pushing back on the management's attempt to introduce a pay cut.

push back (on)
resistirse u oponerse a algo

I think Sonia has **something** against me. **She never wants to talk to me.**

have (something) against
*no gustarte alguien por algún
motivo desconocido*

My idea was shot down **by the panel before I had a chance to explain it to them.**

shoot down
rechazar una idea

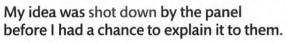

When Emily's boss accused her of being lazy, **she** fought back **by showing him the clothes she had made that morning.**

fight back
*responder a alguien que
te ha criticado*

🔊

43.2 EVITAR EL CONFLICTO

Terry's colleagues always make fun of his shirts, but he just laughs **it off.**

laugh off
*enfrentarse a las críticas o a
una situación difícil riéndote*

Donna bought her brother some chocolates to make up for **the things she had said to him.**

make up for
*hacer algo positivo para enmendar
un error*

Paul usually shrugs off **criticism of his cooking.**

shrug off
*tratar algo como si
no fuera importante*

The two companies have almost reached a deal. They just need to iron out **a few last details.**

iron out
*solucionar pequeños
problemas o detalles*

Everyone criticized Magda's art when she started, but she rose above **it and is a successful artist now.**

rise above
*no dejarte afectar mucho por las
críticas o una situación difícil*

🔊

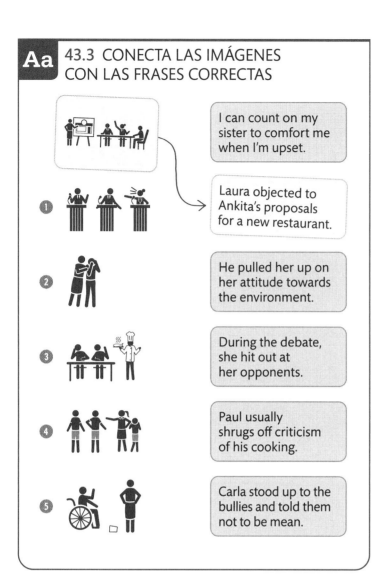

Aa 43.3 CONECTA LAS IMÁGENES CON LAS FRASES CORRECTAS

I can count on my sister to comfort me when I'm upset.

Laura objected to Ankita's proposals for a new restaurant.

He pulled her up on her attitude towards the environment.

During the debate, she hit out at her opponents.

Paul usually shrugs off criticism of his cooking.

Carla stood up to the bullies and told them not to be mean.

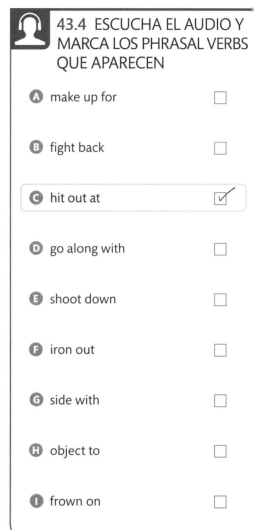

43.4 ESCUCHA EL AUDIO Y MARCA LOS PHRASAL VERBS QUE APARECEN

A make up for ☐

B fight back ☐

C hit out at ☑

D go along with ☐

E shoot down ☐

F iron out ☐

G side with ☐

H object to ☐

I frown on ☐

Aa 43.5 TACHA LAS PALABRAS INCORRECTAS DE CADA FRASE

Paulina always sides ~~up~~ / with / ~~on~~ our boss. It's so irritating!

1 Everyone agrees **with** / **on** / **for** John that Sian should get the job.

2 Everyone criticized Magda's art, but she rose **above** / **for** / **on** it and is a successful artist now.

3 The workers are pushing **up for** / **back on** / **out of** the management's policies.

4 They disagreed **with** / **of** / **on** each other about what color to paint the kitchen.

43.6 LEE LA FRASE Y MARCA EL SIGNIFICADO CORRECTO

Paul usually shrugs off criticism of his cooking.

Paul hace caso de las críticas.	☐
Paul hace caso omiso de las críticas.	☑
Las críticas ayudan a Paul a mejorar.	☐

1 My aunt frowns on people wearing shoes indoors.

Mi tía lo desaprueba.	☐
Mi tía lleva zapatos dentro de casa.	☐
Mi tía nunca lleva zapatos.	☐

2 Paulina always sides with our boss.

Paulina nunca apoya a nuestro jefe.	☐
A Paulina no le gusta nuestro jefe.	☐
Paulina siempre apoya a nuestro jefe.	☐

3 Laura objected to Ankita's proposals.

A Laura le han gustado las propuestas.	☐
Laura ha apoyado las propuestas.	☐
Laura se ha opuesto a las propuestas.	☐

4 Carla stood up to the bullies.

Carla no se defendió.	☐
Carla se defendió.	☐
Carla era una de las abusonas.	☐

5 They just need to iron out a few last details.

Deben solucionar pequeños problemas.	☐
Tienen que crear problemas.	☐
Tienen que evitar problemas.	☐

43.7 VUELVE A ESCRIBIR LAS FRASES CORRIGIENDO LOS ERRORES

My idea was **shot up** by the panel before I had a chance to explain it to them.

My idea was shot down by the panel before I had a chance to explain it to them.

1 I think Sonia **has** something **about** me. She never wants to talk to me.

_____

2 Martin and Simon **disagreed on** each other about what color to paint the kitchen.

_____

3 Our local representative has **come out under** the plans for a new housing development.

_____

4 Donna bought her brother some chocolates to **make up by** the things she had said to him.

_____

5 Terry's colleagues always make fun of his shirts, but he just **laughs** it **over**.

_____

44 Opiniones y discusiones

44.1 OFRECER OPINIONES

Sorry, I'm not sure what you're getting at.

get at
implicar, intentar decir algo de manera indirecta

Anetta is always speaking out about environmental issues.

speak out
dar públicamente la opinión

The professor weighed in on the debate about the new power station.

weigh in on
añadir tu opinión a un debate en curso

The manager laid into the players after they lost another match.

lay into
criticar a alguien con ira

Andy lashed out at someone who dropped litter in the street.

lash out (at)
criticar a alguien con ira

Farah makes sure to base all her arguments on facts.

base on
aportar hechos o argumentos para fundar tu opinión

44.2 UNIRSE A UNA DISCUSIÓN

Only one of my colleagues stuck up for me when my boss criticized my work.

stick up for
defender a alguien o algo

When Dad accused me of lying, Jo backed me up and told him I was telling the truth.

back up
apoyar a alguien mostrándote de acuerdo con él

Moira tried to drag Phil into her argument with the chef.

drag into
hacer que alguien se enzarce en una discusión contra su voluntad

Phil, however, prefered to stay out of it.

stay out of
evitar enzarzarse en una discusión

Ver también:
back up **12** climb down **19** fall out **49**
make up **41**, **52** take back **10**, **16**, **55**

44.3 RENDICIÓN, COMPROMISO Y RECONCILIACIÓN

Ben and Gus finally made up after their argument.

make up (with)
volver a ser amigos

They had fallen out when they both applied for the same job.

fall out (with)
tener un conflicto con alguien

Sam wanted his waiters to dress as hot dogs. He backed down when they threatened to quit.

back down
retirar una exigencia o admitir un error

When Pete showed Martin the facts, Martin had to climb down and admit he was wrong.

climb down (UK)
admitir un error (tras presentar algo de resistencia)

Kirsten had been threatening to fire Imran, but she backed off when he promised to work harder.

back off
retirar una amenaza

Arun and Les patched things up after they had an argument.

patch up
limar asperezas y volver a ser amigos

I'm sorry I said I didn't like your dress, Katie. I take it back.

take back
admitir que lo que dijiste estaba mal

I'm trying to smooth things over with Anna, so I bought her some flowers.

smooth over (with)
resolver un problema o una disputa

Craig's parents finally caved in and bought him a games console.

cave in
aceptar algo (tras presentar mucha resistencia)

Ed hated Carla's new book, but he watered down his opinion when he wrote his review.

water down
rebajar una opinión o una propuesta

44.4 CONECTA LAS DEFINICIONES CON LOS PHRASAL VERBS CORRECTOS

hacer discutir a alguien contra su voluntad

speak out

❶ retirar una amenaza

take back

❷ dar públicamente la opinión

drag into

❸ admitir que lo que dijiste estaba mal

stay out of

❹ evitar enzarzarse en una discusión

base on

❺ limar asperezas y volver a ser amigos

stick up for

❻ aportar hechos o argumentos para fundar tu opinión

back off

❼ defender a alguien o algo

patch up

44.5 ESCUCHA EL AUDIO Y LUEGO NUMERA LAS FRASES EN EL ORDEN EN QUE APARECEN

Ⓐ Anetta is always speaking out about environmental issues. ☐

Ⓑ Arun and Les patched things up after they had an argument. ☐

Ⓒ Ed hated Carla's new book, but he watered down his opinion in his review. ☐ 1

Ⓓ I'm sorry I said I didn't like your dress, Katie. I take it back. ☐

Ⓔ Farah makes sure to base all her arguments on facts. ☐

Ⓕ The professor weighed in on the debate about the new power station. ☐

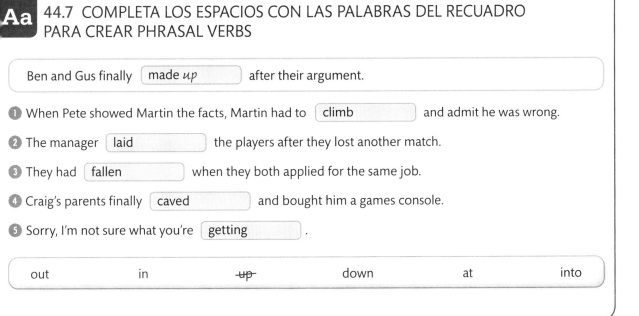

Aa 44.6 ESCRIBE LOS PHRASAL VERBS DEL RECUADRO BAJO LAS DEFINICIONES CORRECTAS

resolver un problema o una disputa

smooth over (with)

❶ retirar una amenaza

_____

❷ evitar enzarzarse en una discusión

_____

❸ apoyar a alguien mostrándote de acuerdo con él

_____

❹ defender a alguien o algo

_____

❺ tener un conflicto con alguien

_____

❻ criticar a alguien con ira

_____

❼ retirar una exigencia o admitir un error

_____

back up	lash out (at)	stick up for	back off
back down	stay out of	~~smooth over (with)~~	fall out (with)

Aa 44.7 COMPLETA LOS ESPACIOS CON LAS PALABRAS DEL RECUADRO PARA CREAR PHRASAL VERBS

Ben and Gus finally [made _up_] after their argument.

❶ When Pete showed Martin the facts, Martin had to [climb] and admit he was wrong.

❷ The manager [laid] the players after they lost another match.

❸ They had [fallen] when they both applied for the same job.

❹ Craig's parents finally [caved] and bought him a games console.

❺ Sorry, I'm not sure what you're [getting] .

out	in	~~up~~	down	at	into

45 Emociones

45.1 EMOCIONES POSITIVAS

The children burst out laughing when the clown pretended to fall over.

burst out
empezar de repente (a reír o llorar)

Yana was upset, but she brightened up when I bought her some tickets to a concert.

brighten up
empezar a sentirse más feliz

Craig had had a bad day at work, but watching a funny movie cheered him up.

cheer up
sentirse más feliz o hacer que alguien se sienta más feliz

Anna hadn't been feeling great, but she perked up after a cup of tea and a cookie.

perk up
sentirse más feliz o animado

45.2 GESTIÓN DE LAS EMOCIONES

When Linda feels stressed, she listens to music to help her calm down.

calm down
calmarse

I really feel for Kim. She's been so upset since her cat went missing.

feel for
sentir empatía por alguien

Cory's daughter started to settle down as he sang her a soothing song.

settle down
calmarse

I've been checking up on Andrei every day since he lost his job. He's been very upset.

check up on
comprobar que alguien está bien

Petra's been sulking for days. I wish she'd snap out of it.

snap out of
mejorar el ánimo o la conducta de repente

Jack's a very private person, but he finally opened up and told me how he feels.

open up
revelar los sentimientos reales

Ver también:
brighten up **11**   calm down **11**   get over **32**, **53**   move on **20**
open up **24**   settle down **2**   turn to **13**, **21**, **50**   work through **20**

Sophie needs to lighten up. She's still studying even though it's her birthday today.

lighten up
dejar de tomárselo todo tan a pecho

Patrick's love of music shines through when he starts playing his guitar.

shine through
*poner de manifiesto, saltar a la vista
(una emoción o cualidad positiva)*

Hiro's jokes are hilarious. He really cracks me up.

crack up
*empezar a reír o hacer que alguien
se ría mucho*

Donny's face lit up when he saw the presents waiting for him on the table.

light up
parecer feliz de repente

Kathy and Jamal broke up last month, but Kathy is still finding it hard to get over it.

get over
recuperarse de una mala experiencia

Kathy is finally moving on after her break up with Jamal last year.

move on
dejar de pensar en alguien o algo

Ed's really toughened up after three years in the army.

toughen up
reforzarse a nivel físico o mental

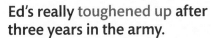

Whenever I'm upset, I know I can turn to my sister.

turn to
pedir ayuda a alguien

I see a therapist to help me work through my problems.

work through
*enfrentarse a los problemas
de forma sistemática*

My therapist has helped me to cope with many of my problems.

cope with
gestionar una situación

Aa 45.3 LEE LA FRASE Y MARCA EL SIGNIFICADO CORRECTO

The children burst out laughing.
De repente dejaron de reírse. ☐
De repente empezaron a reírse. ☑
No se rieron. ☐

1 Ed's toughened up after joining the army.
Ed está más fuerte. ☐
Ed está más débil. ☐
Ed no es bastante fuerte. ☐

2 She has helped me cope with my problems.
Me ha ayudado a crearme problemas. ☐
Me ha ayudado a gestionar mis problemas. ☐
Me ha creado problemas. ☐

3 Kathy is trying to get over her breakup.
Kathy está intentando recuperarse. ☐
Kathy está rompiendo con alguien. ☐
Kathy ha olvidado su ruptura. ☐

4 Anna perked up after a cup of tea.
Anna se ha quedado dormida. ☐
Anna se ha vuelto perezosa. ☐
Anna cada vez es más feliz. ☐

45.4 ESCUCHA EL AUDIO Y CONECTA LAS IMÁGENES CON LOS PHRASAL VERBS CORRECTOS

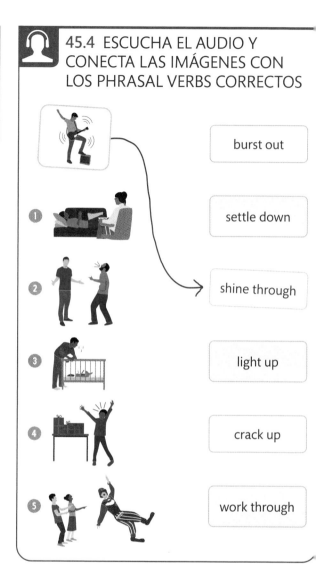

burst out

settle down

shine through

light up

crack up

work through

Aa 45.5 TACHA LAS PALABRAS INCORRECTAS DE CADA FRASE

I see a therapist to help me work ~~under~~ / through / ~~over~~ my problems.

1 Donny's face lit up / out / off when he saw the presents waiting for him on the table.

2 Jack's a very private person, but he finally opened on / up / in and told me how he feels.

3 When Linda feels stressed, she listens to music to help her calm up / down / out.

4 The children burst off / in / out laughing when the clown pretended to fall over.

45.6 COMPLETA LOS ESPACIOS PONIENDO LAS PALABRAS EN SU ORDEN CORRECTO

| down | settle | to |

Cory's daughter started __*to*__ __*settle*__ __*down*__ as he sang her a soothing song.

| up | on | checking |

① I've been _____ _____ _____ Andrei every day since he lost his job.

| up | cheered | him |

② Craig had had a bad day at work, but watching a funny movie _____ _____ _____ .

| up | me | cracks |

③ Hiro's jokes are hilarious. He really _____ _____ _____ .

| when | brightened | up |

④ Yana was upset, but she _____ _____ _____ I bought her tickets to a concert.

45.7 VUELVE A ESCRIBIR LAS FRASES CORRIGIENDO LOS ERRORES

Whenever I'm upset, I know I can **turn around** my sister.
Whenever I'm upset, I know I can turn to my sister.

① Sophie needs to **lighten down**. She's still studying even though it's her birthday today.

_____

② I really **feel about** Kim. She's been so upset since her cat went missing.

_____

③ Kathy is finally **moving off** after her breakup with Jamal last year.

_____

④ Petra's been sulking for days. I wish she'd **snap in of** it.

_____

46 Emociones negativas

46.1 EMOCIONES NEGATIVAS

Chris had been bottling up his emotions for a long time.

bottle up
sentirse incapaz de mostrar las emociones a otros

He eventually broke down and admitted that he was really upset.

break down
romper a llorar

Andy fell apart when I told him that I was moving to another country.

fall apart
ponerse muy sensible, perder el control

This song is so moving. It always sets me off.

set off
hacer llorar a alguien

It really gets to me when people leave their trash on the metro.

get to
irritar o molestar a alguien

Tamal and Sam choked up when the hero died at the end of the movie.

choke up
ponerse sensible o enojarse

I'm sick of my neighbors arguing. It's been getting me down for months.

get down
hacer deprimir a alguien

Bella welled up when Pete asked her to marry him.

well up
llenarse los ojos de lágrimas, romper a llorar

Stop taking it out on me. It's not my fault the weather is awful.

take out on
portarse mal con alguien a pesar de que no tenga la culpa

When Lisa walked onto the stage she froze up. She couldn't say anything!

freeze up
ser incapaz de comunicarse de repente

Ver también:
break down **9**, **50**   fall apart **49**   get down **19**, **53**
get to **53**   set off **35**, **53**

Sadie's anger about her boss's rude behavior had been building up.

build up
aumentar o reforzarse

It eventually spilled over, and Sadie told her how she felt.

spill over
empezar a mostrar
(de manera incontrolada)

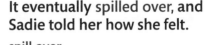

Simone's eyes misted over as she told me about her childhood in the countryside.

mist over
(los ojos) llenarse de lágrimas

Clare flew into a rage when her computer crashed and lost all her work.

fly into
(genio, ira o pánico) enfadarse
o asustarse mucho de repente

My husband tenses up whenever I try to talk about money with him.

tense up
ponerse tenso o ansioso de repente

Troy freaked out when he noticed the enormous spider climbing up the wall.

freak out
enfadarse o asustarse mucho (informal)

My grandchildren love to wind me up. They're always playing tricks on me.

wind up (UK)
tomarle el pelo a alguien,
hacer que alguien se enfade

Work has been weighing on me a lot recently.

weigh on
hacer que alguien se preocupe

My manager is usually very understanding, but he blew up when I told him that I'd left my work laptop on the train.

blow up
enfadarse mucho de repente

Aa 46.2 CONECTA LOS PRINCIPIOS DE LAS FRASES CON LOS FINALES CORRECTOS

It really gets to me when

1 My husband tenses up whenever

2 This song is so moving.

3 Troy freaked out when he noticed

4 Clare flew into a rage when

5 Stop taking it out on me.

6 My grandchildren love to wind me up.

I try to talk about money with him.

her computer crashed and lost all her work.

They're always playing tricks on me.

people leave their trash on the metro.

the enormous spider climbing up the wall.

It always sets me off.

It's not my fault the weather is awful.

46.3 ESCUCHA EL AUDIO Y COMPLETA LAS FRASES QUE DESCRIBEN LAS IMÁGENES

Simone's eyes ___*misted over*___ as she told me about her childhood in the countryside.

1 Sadie's anger about her boss's rude behavior had been _____ .

2 Tamal and Sam _____ when the hero died at the end of the movie.

3 When Lisa walked onto the stage she _____ . She couldn't say anything!

4 He eventually _____ and admitted that he was really upset.

5 My manager _____ when I told him that I'd left my work laptop on the train.

Aa 46.4 MIRA LAS IMÁGENES Y COMPLETA LAS FRASES CON PHRASAL VERBS DEL RECUADRO

Andy _____*fell apart*_____ when I told him that I was moving to another country.

③ Chris had been _____ his emotions for a long time.

① Bella _____ when Pete asked her to marry him.

④ Work has been _____ me a lot recently.

② It eventually _____ , and Sadie told her how she felt.

⑤ Clare _____ a rage when her computer crashed and lost all her work.

| spilled over | flew into | ~~fell apart~~ | bottling up | welled up | weighing on |

Aa 46.5 ESCRIBE EL PHRASAL VERB CORRECTO AL LADO DE SU DEFINICIÓN COMPLETANDO LAS LETRAS QUE FALTAN

hacer llorar a alguien	=	s e t o f f
① hacer deprimir a alguien	=	g _ _ _ d _ _ _ _
② tomarle el pelo a alguien, hacer que se enfade	=	w _ _ _ _ u _
③ romper a llorar	=	b _ _ _ _ _ d _ _ _ _
④ enfadarse mucho de repente	=	b _ _ _ _ u _

47 Tomar decisiones

47.1 TOMAR DECISIONES

Lisa found it hard to choose a dress, but eventually decided on the red one.

decide on
alcanzar una decisión

After a lot of thought, Rob went for the fish instead of the steak.

go for
elegir

Moving to New Zealand next year hinges on us saving enough money.

hinge on
depender por completo de algo

It's so hard to choose! I'm leaning toward the red sports car.

lean toward
ser más probable una opción que otra

Marie didn't know which new job to accept, so she decided to sleep on it.

sleep on
esperar hasta el día siguiente para tomar una decisión

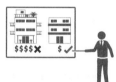

Shona regrets her decision to quit, but she's going to have to live with it.

live with
aceptar una decisión o situación incómoda

We loved your plans for the new apartment block. But our decision came down to funding.

come down to
depender de un punto

After so many failures, Stephen's banking on this new recipe to impress his guests.

bank on
depender de

We were sure our café would be a success, but forgot to factor in the local competition.

factor in
tener en cuenta

Ver también:
arrive at **35** go for **54** live with **2**

Can you tell us how you settled on a winner?

We arrived at our decision after looking carefully at each of the paintings.

settle on
decidir (tras pensarlo o debatirlo)

arrive at
alcanzar, llegar a una decisión

The workers wanted a 5% pay raise, but eventually settled for 3%.

settle for
acordar algo a pesar de no ser lo que se quería al principio

Yasmin has been toying with the idea of getting her hair cut short, but has never done it.

toy with
tener en cuenta, barajar una idea

Paula weighed up her options before deciding which camera to buy.

weigh up
considerar los aspectos positivos y negativos antes de tomar una decisión

Somrita has been mulling over which candidate to hire.

mull over
pensar en algo un tiempo antes de tomar una decisión

Ahmed's betting on it being a hot summer this year so he's bought an ice-cream van.

bet on
actuar según una esperanza o predicción

We have narrowed down our list of potential homes to two properties.

narrow down
reducir el número de opciones

Sonia opted out of the boat trip. She always gets sea sick.

opt out (of)
elegir no hacer algo

Archie picked out the toy he wanted for his birthday.

pick out
elegir con cuidado entre un grupo

Aa 47.2 TACHA LAS PALABRAS INCORRECTAS DE CADA FRASE

 Somrita has been mulling ~~in~~ / over / ~~on~~ which candidate to hire.

1 Sonia opted over / on / out of the boat trip. She always gets sea sick.

2 Yasmin has been toying on / with / to the idea of getting her hair cut short.

3 The workers wanted a 5% pay raise, but settled out / for / in 3%.

4 Shona regrets her decision to quit, but she's going to have to live with / in / on it.

5 After a lot of thought, Rob went on / out / for the fish instead of the steak.

Aa 47.3 CONECTA LAS DEFINICIONES CON LOS PHRASAL VERBS CORRECTOS

depender por completo de algo → decide on

1 alcanzar una decisión — opt out

2 tener en cuenta — hinge on

3 pensar en algo antes de tomar una decisión — pick out

4 elegir con cuidado entre un grupo — factor in

5 elegir no hacer algo — lean toward

6 ser más probable una opción que otra — mull over

47.4 ESCUCHA EL AUDIO Y MARCA LOS PHRASAL VERBS QUE APARECEN

bet on ☑
bet in ☐

1 weigh up ☐
weigh out ☐

2 narrow down ☐
narrow up ☐

3 pick over ☐
pick out ☐

4 sleep on ☐
sleep in ☐

5 lean toward ☐
lean on ☐

Aa 47.5 COMPLETA LOS ESPACIOS PONIENDO LAS PALABRAS EN SU ORDEN CORRECTO

| up | weighed | her |

Paula __weighed__ __up__ __her__ options before deciding which camera to buy.

| on | us | hinges |

1 Moving to New Zealand next year _____ _____ _____ saving enough money.

| on | settled | a |

2 Can you tell us how you _____ _____ _____ winner?

| decided | the | on |

3 Lisa found it hard to choose a dress, but eventually _____ _____ _____ red one.

| this | on | banking |

4 Stephen is _____ _____ _____ new recipe to impress his guests.

48 Cometer errores

48.1 COMETER ERRORES

Coralie's graph didn't make sense, so she looked through the data again to see where she'd slipped up.

slip up
cometer un error

I'll never live down the time I dropped Erin's birthday cake in the middle of her party.

live down
hacer que la gente se olvide de un error garrafal que cometiste

Wang thought he'd bought everyone a drink until he noticed he'd missed Ellie out.

miss out
olvidarse de incluir a alguien o algo en una actividad

Tariq landed himself in trouble when he forgot to do his homework.

land in
meterse en una mala situación

When Juan missed the penalty, his teammates rubbed it in by laughing at him.

rub in
hacer que alguien se sienta mal por un error o un fallo

When Chris got home from work, he realized that he had mixed his bag up with Simon's.

mix up (with)
confundir algo por otra cosa por accidente

I was relying on Selma to bring candles for the cake, but she let me down.

let down
no cumplir las expectativas o no conseguir mantener una promesa

Enzo went back to the café when he realized he'd left his wallet behind.

leave behind
olvidarse de llevar a alguien o algo contigo

The spelling mistake in Juanita's homework jumped out at me.

jump out at
ser obvio para alguien

I crossed out the misspelled word and wrote it again correctly.

cross out
tachar una palabra

48.2 ESCUCHA EL AUDIO Y LUEGO NUMERA LAS FRASES EN EL ORDEN EN QUE APARECEN

A Enzo went back to the café when he realized he'd left his wallet behind. ☐

B Tariq landed himself in trouble when he forgot to do his homework. ☐

C When Juan missed the penalty, his teammates rubbed it in by laughing at him. ☐1

D I crossed out the misspelled word and wrote it again correctly. ☐

E The spelling mistake in Juanita's homework jumped out at me. ☐

Aa 48.3 VUELVE A ESCRIBIR LAS FRASES CORRIGIENDO LOS ERRORES

Jimish thought he'd bought everyone a drink until he noticed he'd **missed** Ellie **on**.
Jimish thought he'd bought everyone a drink until he noticed he'd missed Ellie out.

❶ I was relying on Selma to bring candles for the cake, but she **letting** me **down**.
_____

❷ I'll never **die down** the time I dropped Erin's birthday cake in the middle of her party.
_____

❸ Coralie's graph didn't make sense, so she looked through the data again to see where she'd **slipping up**.
_____

❹ When Chris got home from work, he realized that he had **mixed** his bag **up for** Simon's.
_____

❺ The spelling mistake in Juanita's homework **pounced out at** me.
_____

49 Accidentes y daños

49.1 ACCIDENTES

Chrissy accidentally broke the handle off **the antique vase.**

break off
separar con fuerza

The old book came apart in the **librarian's hands.**

come apart
caerse a trozos

The dog knocked over **the plant pot as it chased the cat.**

knock over
*chocar contra algo
y tirarlo al suelo*

The hairdresser has completely messed up **Kira's hair. She's furious about it.**

mess up
*dejar algo desaliñado o desaseado,
hacer algo incorrectamente*

I banged into **the door while leaving the house.**

bang into
chocar contra alguien o algo sin querer

Takira tripped over **one of her son's toys.**

trip over
tropezar con algo y caerse al suelo

49.3 PHRASAL VERBS CON "FALL"

When Omar fell over **in the backyard, his dad rushed over to help him.**

fall over
*caerse al suelo cuando
se estaba de pie*

The old manor house Andrei wants to buy looks as if it's about to fall down.

fall down
estar en muy mal estado, caerse por momentos (un edificio)

Rodrigo slammed the door so hard that the pictures fell off **the wall.**

fall off
*caer al suelo desde
un lugar más elevado*

Ver también:
break off **30**   fall apart **46**
fall out **44**   wear out **33**

49.2 DAÑOS

When I got home, I found that the dog had torn a cushion apart.

tear apart
destruir algo despedazándolo

After her favorite band split up, Jo tore up all her posters of them.

tear up
romper algo a tiras, rasgar

Colin accidentally drove into a tree and smashed up his van.

smash up
romper algo

The drain was clogged up with old leaves, so I had to unblock it.

clog up
quedar atascado

My son has worn out another pair of shoes!

wear out
utilizar algo mucho hasta el punto de no poder utilizarlo más

Jorge took the old clock apart to fix it.

take apart
desmontar algo, separarlo en piezas

Sanjay's old car is falling apart. He's had it since he was a teenager.

fall apart
romperse algo (de viejo o por mala calidad)

David's wallet fell out of his pocket while he was running for the bus.

fall out (of)
caerse de un sitio cerrado

After the leak in the room above, it looked like the ceiling might fall in.

fall in
derrumbarse y caer al suelo

Aa 49.4 MARCA LAS FRASES CORRECTAS

My son has worn out another pair of shoes! ☑
My son has worn off another pair of shoes! ☐

1 After the leak in the room above, it looked like the ceiling might fall in. ☐
After the leak in the room above, it looked like the ceiling might fall on. ☐

2 The dog knocked out the plant pot as it chased the cat. ☐
The dog knocked over the plant pot as it chased the cat. ☐

3 Jorge took the old clock under to fix it. ☐
Jorge took the old clock apart to fix it. ☐

4 When I got home, I found that the dog had torn a cushion apart. ☐
When I got home, I found that the dog had torn a cushion aside. ☐

49.5 ESCUCHA EL AUDIO Y LUEGO NUMERA LAS IMÁGENES EN EL ORDEN EN QUE APARECEN

A ☐   B 1
C ☐   D ☐
E ☐   F ☐

Aa 49.6 CONECTA LOS VERBOS CON LAS PARTÍCULAS CORRECTAS PARA CONSTRUIR PHRASAL VERBS

clog — out
1 smash — over
2 wear → up
3 bang — off
4 trip — up
5 fall — into
6 break — in

David's wallet ___*fell out of*___ his pocket while he was running for the bus.

④ The old book _____ in the librarian's hands.

① I _____ the door while leaving the house.

⑤ The drain was _____with old leaves, so I had to unblock it.

② Colin accidentally drove into a tree and _____ his van.

⑥ Sanjay's old car is _____. He's had it since he was a teenager.

③ Rodrigo slammed the door so hard that the pictures _____ the wall.

⑦ The old manor house Andrei wants to buy looks as if it's about to _____.

came apart	fall down	fell off	banged into
falling apart	~~fell out of~~	smashed up	clogged up

203

50.1 PROBLEMAS Y SOLUCIONES

Sorry, I'll be home late tonight. Something's come up.

come up
pasar de manera inesperada

Writing your thesis is easier if you break it down into small sections.

break down
hacer algo más fácil de entender dividiéndolo en partes más pequeñas

The proposals for a new highway have come up against a lot of local opposition.

come up against
encontrar dificultades

I thought the event was going to be a disaster, but it turned out alright.

turn out
suceder algo diferente a lo esperado

It was very hard for Somrita and her friends to relax with their final exams hanging over them.

hang over
ser motivo de preocupación

Owen is great with customers. He deals with their complaints fairly, and never loses his temper.

deal with
gestionar o solucionar un problema

While climbing the mountain, we had to contend with strong winds and heavy rain.

contend with
lidiar con dificultades u oposición

Ben and I cleared up our disagreement when we realized it was all just a misunderstanding.

clear up
solucionar un problema, resolver una discusión

A number of problems have cropped up with the new printer. We need to get someone to fix it.

crop up
suceder (a menudo de manera inesperada)

Bitna told Danny she was nervous about her presentation, but he just brushed it aside.

brush aside
tratar un problema como si fuera nimio, no querer tomárselo en serio

Ver también: break down **9**, **46**   call in **4**, **22**   check out **10**, **35**
clear up **11**, **32**   come up **16**, **36**, **52**   get around **35**, **53**
think through **39**   turn to **13**, **21**, **45**

Clare and Wei Ting had to sort out a problem with their experiment.

sort out
solucionar un problema

They stayed up late to thrash it out and find a solution.

thrash out
hablar de un problema
para solucionarlo

Sawad's computer crashed, but she worked around it by using pen and paper instead.

work around
evitar un obstáculo que te impide
conseguir algo

Kavitha didn't know why her equation was wrong, so she thought it through carefully.

think through
considerar algo de manera metódica

Anton had run out of green paint, but he managed to get around it.

get around
evitar o solucionar un problema
u obstáculo

It's taken me all evening to figure out how to turn on this new television.

figure out
solucionar un problema

Femmy's thinking of moving to a new part of town, so she went to check out the area.

check out
mirar si alguien o algo
es aceptable

One of the pipes was leaking, so we called in a plumber to fix it.

call in
pedir a una persona capacitada
que te gestione un problema

Whenever Gitanjali has a problem, she turns to her grandmother for advice.

turn to
ir a pedir ayuda o consejo
a alguien

🔊

50.2 ESCUCHA EL AUDIO Y LUEGO NUMERA LAS IMÁGENES EN EL ORDEN EN QUE APARECEN

A ☐

B ☐ 1

C ☐

D ☐

E ☐

F ☐

G ☐

H ☐

Aa 50.3 CONECTA LAS FRASES QUE SIGNIFICAN LO MISMO

Clare and Wei Ting had to sort out a problem with their experiment.

While climbing the mountain, we had to deal with strong winds and heavy rain.

1 Whenever Gitanjali has a problem, she turns to her grandmother for advice.

Clare and Wei Ting had to find a solution to a problem with their experiment.

2 While climbing the mountain, we had to contend with strong winds and heavy rain.

It's taken me all evening to find out how to turn on this new television.

3 The proposals for a new highway have come up against a lot of local opposition.

One of the pipes was leaking, so we asked a plumber to fix it.

4 One of the pipes was leaking, so we called in a plumber to fix it.

Whenever Gitanjali has a problem, she goes to her grandmother for advice.

5 Writing your thesis is easier if you break it down into small sections.

The proposals for a new highway have encountered a lot of local opposition.

6 It's taken me all evening to figure out how to turn on this new television.

Writing your thesis is easier if you separate it into small sections.

Aa 50.4 ESCRIBE LOS PHRASAL VERBS DEL RECUADRO EN LOS GRUPOS CORRECTOS

SEPARABLES	INSEPARABLES
	turn to

come up against   break down   crop up   thrash out

brush aside   get around   think through   ~~turn to~~

Aa 50.5 ESCRIBE LOS PHRASAL VERBS DEL RECUADRO BAJO LAS DEFINICIONES CORRECTAS

evitar o solucionar un problema u obstáculo
get around

❶ suceder algo diferente a lo esperado

❷ considerar algo de manera metódica

❸ solucionar un problema

❹ solucionar un problema, resolver una discusión

❺ tratar un problema como si fuera nimio, no querer tomárselo en serio

❻ pedir a una persona capacitada que te gestione un problema

❼ mirar si alguien o algo es aceptable

sort out   check out   think through   brush aside

turn out   ~~get around~~   clear up   thrash out

51 Secretos y sorpresas

51.1 SECRETOS

Jessica has been keeping the name of her new boyfriend from me.

keep from
no decirle algo a alguien

Paolo has prepared a new sculpture for the exhibition. I've asked him what it is, but he's not giving anything away!

give away
revelar un secreto

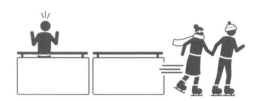

I only cottoned onto the fact that Lisa and Pete were dating when I saw them at the ice rink together.

cotton on(to) (UK)
empezar a entender o darse cuenta de algo

51.2 SORPRESAS

We were all eating our dinner when the dog burst into the room.

burst in(to)
entrar en una habitación o edificio de repente

I was bowled over when Nadia announced that she had been accepted into dance school.

bowl over
encantar o impresionar a alguien

Kamal was blown away by Jose's account of his adventures in the Amazon.

blow away
causar una impresión apabullante (informal)

Mollie crept up on her grandfather while he slept in the garden.

creep up on
acercarse a alguien sigilosamente para sorprenderle

My best friend sprang it on me last night that she's moving to Canada.

spring on
anunciar algo sin previo aviso

The surprising news was a lot to take in.

take in
entender o aceptar determinadas noticias o informaciones

Ver también:
blurt out **36**   creep up on **15**   give away **55**
keep from **33**   slip out **5**   take in **6, 55**

My little sister blurted out to Dad that we'd organized a surprise party for him. She can't keep a secret.

blurt out
decir algo de repente, sin pensarlo

I didn't mean to tell the team that it was your birthday. It just slipped out.

slip out
decir algo por error

The movie star tried to hush up the fact that she had a new boyfriend.

hush up
ocultar la verdad

Clara can't believe she passed her medical exams. It's going to take a while for it to sink in.

sink in
entender por completo

My daughter often pretends to be a dinosaur. We all have to play along with her.

play along
fingir que algo es verdad o que te crees algo

People have woken up to the fact that we need to look after the environment.

wake up to
darse cuenta de la importancia de algo

While I was on vacation in Venice, I bumped into one of my cousins. I couldn't believe it.

bump into
encontrarse con alguien de manera inesperada

I was shopping at the antiques market when I stumbled upon a valuable necklace.

stumble upon
encontrar por casualidad

I was taken aback when Tia and Juan told me they were getting married.

take aback
sorprender a alguien

Aa 51.3 CONECTA EL PRINCIPIO Y EL FINAL DE CADA FRASE

Kamal was blown away by Jose's → account of his adventures in the Amazon.

that it was your birthday. It just slipped out.

that she had been accepted into dance school.

1 I didn't mean to tell the team

2 The movie star tried to hush up

while he slept in the garden.

3 Jessica has been keeping

the fact that she had a new boyfriend.

4 I was bowled over when Nadia announced

the name of her new boyfriend from me.

5 Mollie crept up on her grandfather

Aa 51.4 TACHA LAS PALABRAS INCORRECTAS DE CADA FRASE

 We were all eating our dinner when the dog burst ~~onto~~ / into / ~~through~~ the room.

1 Clara can't believe she passed her exams. It's going to take a while for it to sink **down / of / in**.

2 People have woken **for / up / of** to the fact that we need to look after the environment.

3 I was shopping at the antiques market when I stumbled **over / upon / in** a valuable necklace.

4 My best friend **sprang / jumped / splashed** it on me last night that she's moving to Canada.

5 I was taken **about / aback / around** when Tia and Juan told me they were getting married.

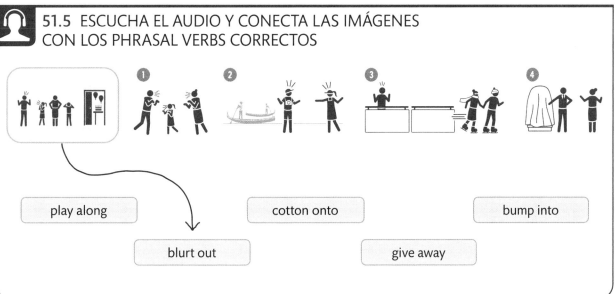

51.5 ESCUCHA EL AUDIO Y CONECTA LAS IMÁGENES CON LOS PHRASAL VERBS CORRECTOS

play along

cotton onto

bump into

blurt out

give away

Aa 51.6 VUELVE A ESCRIBIR LAS FRASES PONIENDO LAS PALABRAS EN SU ORDEN CORRECTO

surprising | lot | was | The | to | take | in. | news | a

The surprising news was a lot to take in.

a | the | stumbled | valuable | market. | I | necklace | upon | at | antiques

① _____

keeping | Jessica | the | me. | new | has | name | boyfriend | her | been | of | from

② _____

on | grandfather | crept | her | up | in | slept | he | the | Mollie | while | garden.

③ _____

room. | the | We | our | were | dinner | burst | into | eating | when | dog | the

④ _____

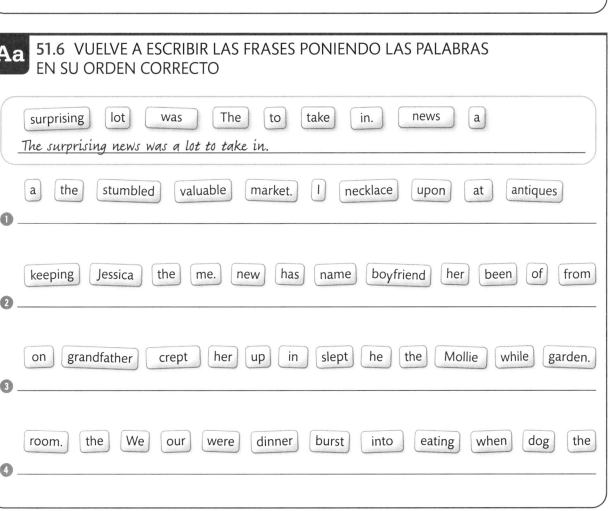

52 "Come," "make" y "do"

52.1 PHRASAL VERBS CON "COME"

Hetty's career as a musician came about after a producer saw her performing.

come about
suceder (a menudo sin planificarlo)

When I tried to log into my account, a message came up saying that my account had been blocked.

come up
aparecer (en la pantalla)

Staying in touch with friends became much easier once the internet came along.

come along
aparecer, estar disponible, existir

Ben and Eleanor came out of the toy store with presents for their grandchildren.

come out (of)
abandonar una habitación, edificio o espacio cerrado

Natsuo came across the room to speak to us.

come across
cruzar una habitación, espacio, país, etc.

The company has come under attack for its high carbon emissions.

come under
experimentar algo negativo (como críticas, amenazas o ataques)

Derek sat down in front of the TV when the ten o'clock news came on.

come on
empezar (un programa de televisión)

My daughter's still waiting for her results to come through. She's so nervous.

come through
llegar (noticias o información)

No matter how much we clean it, this graffiti won't come off the wall.

come off
sacar

Ver también: come across **1**, **39**   come along **5**, **31**   come off **6**, **26**
come on **27**, **56**   come out (of) **6**   come up **16**, **36**, **50**   do up **52**
make for **37**   make out **41**   make up **41**, **44**

52.2 PHRASAL VERBS CON "MAKE"

Lots of talented people make up our circus's team of acrobats.

make up
constituir, formar algo

Luanne struggled to make out what the train conductor was saying.

make out
conseguir ver, oír o entender

We were about to eat dinner when the dog made off with the leg of lamb.

make off with
huir con algo

With hot weather expected, thousands of tourists made for the coast.

make for
ir hacia un sitio

When I asked Kim what she made of Toshi's new novel, she said she loved it.

make of
tener opinión sobre algo

🔊

52.3 PHRASAL VERBS CON "DO"

Emily is doing up her house at the moment. It's going to look great when she's finished.

do up
mejorar, renovar

With so many people using bank cards, we may be able to do away with cash in the future.

do away with
eliminar, no hacer falta

The council needs to decide what it's going to do about the city's litter problem.

do about
hacer algo para solucionar un problema

Riya was very disappointed with her wedding cake, and insisted it be done over.

do over (US)
volver a hacer algo

🔊

213

52.4 CONECTA LOS PHRASAL VERBS CON LAS DEFINICIONES CORRECTAS

do up	sacar
① come off	tener opinión sobre algo
② come up	mejorar, renovar
③ do about	aparecer (en la pantalla)
④ make of	huir con algo
⑤ make for	eliminar, no hacer falta
⑥ make off with	ir hacia un lugar
⑦ do away with	hacer algo para solucionar un problema

52.5 ESCUCHA EL AUDIO Y LUEGO NUMERA LAS FRASES EN EL ORDEN EN QUE APARECEN

Ⓐ Natsuo came across the room to speak to us. ☐

Ⓑ We were about to eat dinner when the dog made off with the leg of lamb. ☐

Ⓒ Ben and Eleanor came out of the toy store with presents for their grandchildren. [1]

Ⓓ My daughter's still waiting for her results to come through. She's so nervous. ☐

Ⓔ When I asked Kim what she made of Toshi's new novel, she said she loved it. ☐

Ⓕ Staying in touch with friends became much easier once the internet came along. ☐

52.6 COMPLETA LOS ESPACIOS CON LOS PHRASAL VERBS DEL RECUADRO

The company has _come under_ attack for its high carbon emissions.

1. Riya was disappointed with her wedding cake, and insisted it be _____ .

2. With hot weather expected, thousands of tourists _____ the coast.

3. Lots of talented people _____ our circus's team of acrobats.

4. Natsuo _____ the room to speak to us.

5. The council has to decide what it's going to _____ the litter problem.

6. Luanne struggled to _____ what the train conductor was saying.

7. No matter how much we clean it, this graffiti won't _____ the wall.

do about

came across

made for

~~come under~~

make out

make up

come off

done over

Aa 52.7 MIRA LAS IMÁGENES Y COMPLETA LAS FRASES CON PHRASAL VERBS

Emily is _doing up_ her house at the moment. It's going to look great when she's finished.

3. Luanne struggled to _____ what the train conductor was saying.

1. Hetty's career as a musician _____ after a producer saw her performing.

4. When I tried to log in, a message _____ saying that my account had been blocked.

2. Derek sat down in front of the TV when the ten o'clock news _____ .

5. Lots of talented people _____ our circus's team of acrobats.

53 "Get" y "set"

53.1 PHRASAL VERBS CON "GET"

Claude got up from his chair and went to make some more tea.

get up (from)
ponerse de pie (estando sentado)

Let's just clean the kitchen now and get it over with.

get over with
completar una tarea que no quieres hacer

It's almost eleven o'clock. We should get down to work.

get down to
empezar a centrarse en una tarea

Can you help me get the shopping in, please?

get in
entrar algo

Chad's oven had broken, but he got around it by using the microwave instead.

get around
evitar un obstáculo, afrontar un problema

Cheryl's dog keeps getting over the fence into the neighbor's backyard.

get over
salvar un obstáculo por encima

53.2 PHRASAL VERBS CON "SET"

Harry burned the dinner and set off the smoke detector.

set off
activar, hacer que algo empiece a funcionar

As Martin walked home late at night, fear began to set in.

set in
empezar (algo desagradable que puede durar bastante)

The bad weather has set us back by two weeks. We won't finish building the bridge until November.

set back
costar tiempo, dinero o progreso

Ver también: get around **35**, **50**   get down **19**, **46**   get in **8**, **9**
get out **9**, **56**   get over **32**, **45**   get to **46**   get together **5**
get up **8**   set off **35**, **46**   set out **23**, **35**   set up **3**, **12**

Lee got his fishing rod out of the garage and carried it to his car.

get out (of)
sacar algo (de una bolsa, caja, habitación, etc.)

Ramona always gets her message across, even when she's explaining complicated scientific theories.

get across
conseguir comunicar un mensaje

Glen climbed the ladder to get the cat down from the tree.

get down (from)
recuperar algo de una posición más elevada

Before accusing Simon, the police had to get their facts together.

get together
organizar información o pertenencias

As soon as we got to the ski resort, we went straight to the slopes.

get to
llegar

After Gia was rude to me, I got back at her by not inviting her to my wedding.

get back at
vengarse de alguien

Lee's speed sets him apart from the other players in the tournament.

set apart (from)
hacer alguien o algo especial en comparación con otros

The security guard threatened to set his dog on us if we didn't leave immediately.

set on
ordenarle a alguien o a algo que ataque a alguien más

After leaving school, Romesh set up his own business selling surfboards.

set up
fundar (una empresa)

Mary set out all her qualifications and experience in her resume.

set out
explicar información con detalle

53.3 ESCUCHA EL AUDIO Y COMPLETA LAS FRASES QUE DESCRIBEN LAS IMÁGENES

Claude __*got up from*__ his chair and went to make some more tea.

1. Cheryl's dog keeps _____ the fence into the neighbor's backyard.

2. Harry burned the dinner and _____ the smoke detector.

3. As Martin walked home late at night, fear began to _____ .

4. It's almost eleven o'clock. We should _____ work.

5. Mary _____ all her qualifications and experience in her resume.

6. Lee's speed _____ the other players in the tournament.

Aa 53.4 ESCRIBE LOS PHRASAL VERBS DEL RECUADRO EN LOS GRUPOS CORRECTOS

SEPARABLES	INSEPARABLES
_____	*get around*
_____	_____
_____	_____
_____	_____

get up (from)　　set back　　get to　　set on　　~~get around~~　　get across　　set in　　get together

Aa 53.5 CONECTA LAS DEFINICIONES CON LOS PHRASAL VERBS CORRECTOS

evitar un obstáculo, afrontar un problema	get to
1 ordenarle a alguien o a algo que ataque a alguien más	get across
2 llegar	get around
3 costar tiempo, dinero o progreso	set on
4 vengarse de alguien	get together
5 conseguir comunicar un mensaje	set back
6 organizar información o pertenencias	set up
7 fundar (una empresa)	get back at

Aa 53.6 VUELVE A ESCRIBIR LAS FRASES CORRIGIENDO LOS ERRORES

Let's just clean the kitchen now and **set** it **over with**.
Let's just clean the kitchen now and get it over with.

1 Lee **got** his fishing rod **up of** the garage and carried it to his car.

2 The security guard threatened to **get** his dog **on** us if we didn't leave immediately.

3 Can you help me **got** the shopping **in**, please?

4 Before accusing Simon, the police had to **get** their facts **up**.

5 As soon as we **gotten to** the ski resort, we went straight to the slopes.

54 "Go"

54.1 PHRASAL VERBS CON "GO"

How are you going to go about fixing this car?

go about
empezar a afrontar un problema o una tarea

As soon as I realized Orla had forgotten her bag, I went after her.

go after
seguir o perseguir a alguien

James went over the company's accounts to check for mistakes.

go over
revisar

My daughter goes to ballet classes every Saturday morning.

go to
asistir de manera regular

After I got back from the dentist, it took a couple of hours for the pain to go away.

go away
desaparecer

Michelle and I go back years. I've known her since kindergarten.

go back
conocer a alguien desde hace mucho

Buying water in plastic bottles goes against my principles.

go against
ser lo contrario de lo que deseas o crees

The children watched the hot-air balloon slowly go up into the air.

go up
subir, pasar de una posición más baja a otra más elevada

A team of firefighters went into the burning building.

go in(to)
entrar en un edificio, habitación o espacio cerrado

As soon as the teacher had gone out of the room, the children began misbehaving.

go out (of)
abandonar una habitación, edificio o espacio cerrado

Ver también:
go ahead **56**   go around **32**   go away **56**   go back **16**, **35**   go by **15**
go down **12**, **32**   go for **47**   go out **3**, **5**, **27**   go through **19**

Help yourself to some cakes.
There are enough to go around.

go around
haber suficiente para todos

Malachai went through **a period of
unhappiness after his dog died.**

go through
experimentar algo

There's something going on **next door.
I can hear loud music.**

go on
suceder

Parents often have to go without **sleep
when they have a new baby.**

go without
vivir sin algo

**Cath couldn't find the recipe, so she had to
make it up as she** went along.

go along
continuar haciendo algo

**My new trainer is called Zachariah,
though he usually** goes by **Zac.**

go by
ser conocido por un nombre concreto

Kelly's decided to go for **the job at
the software company. It's
very well paid.**

go for
intentar conseguir algo

All the money we make today will
go toward **funding the
new school library.**

go toward
contribuir

**Rob and I sat on the beach watching
the sun** go down.

go down
*pasar de una posición más
elevada a otra más baja*

**Even though it was a cloudy day, Ramon
decided to** go ahead with **the picnic.**

go ahead (with)
*decidir hacer algo (tras considerarlo
u obtener una aprobación oficial)*

Aa 54.2 CONECTA LAS FRASES QUE SIGNIFICAN LO MISMO

As soon as the teacher had gone out of the room, the children began misbehaving.

After I got back from the dentist, it took a couple of hours for the pain to disappear.

① My daughter goes to ballet classes every Saturday morning.

As soon as the teacher had left the room, the children began misbehaving.

② There's something going on next door. I can hear loud music.

Help yourself to some cakes. There are enough for everyone.

③ James went over the company's accounts to check for mistakes.

My daughter attends ballet classes every Saturday morning.

④ Help yourself to some cakes. There are enough to go around.

Malachai experienced a period of unhappiness after his dog died.

⑤ Malachai went through a period of unhappiness after his dog died.

James reviewed the company's accounts to check for mistakes.

⑥ After I got back from the dentist, it took a couple of hours for the pain to go away.

There's something happening next door. I can hear loud music.

54.3 ESCUCHA EL AUDIO Y LUEGO NUMERA LAS IMÁGENES EN EL ORDEN EN QUE APARECEN

 **A** ☐

 **B** 1

 **C** ☐

 **D** ☐

 **E** ☐

 **F** ☐

 **G** ☐

 **H** ☐

Aa 54.4 MARCA LAS FRASES CORRECTAS

How are you going to go about fixing this car? ☑
How are you going to go above fixing this car? ☐

1 Michelle and I go back years. I've known her since kindergarten. ☐
Michelle and I go up years. I've known her since kindergarten. ☐

2 My new trainer is called Zachariah, though he usually goes by Zac. ☐
My new trainer is called Zachariah, though he usually went by Zac. ☐

3 Buying water in plastic bottles goes against my principles. ☐
Buying water in plastic bottles going against my principles. ☐

4 As soon as I realized Orla had forgotten her bag, I went after her. ☐
As soon as I realized Orla had forgotten her bag, I went before her. ☐

5 The children watched the hot-air balloon slowly went up into the air. ☐
The children watched the hot-air balloon slowly go up into the air. ☐

Aa 54.5 TACHA LAS PALABRAS INCORRECTAS DE CADA FRASE

Cath couldn't find the recipe, so she had to make it up as she went ~~through~~ / ~~on~~ / along.

1 Parents often have to **leave** / **go** / **arrive** without sleep when they have a new baby.

2 Help yourself to some cakes. There are enough to go **among** / **over** / **around**.

3 Kelly's decided to go **for** / **on** / **to** the job at the software company. It's very well paid.

4 Rob and I sat on the beach watching the sun **set** / **go** / **back** down.

5 A team of firefighters went **onto** / **down** / **into** the burning building.

6 All the money we make today will go **forward** / **toward** / **into** funding the new school library.

7 Even though it was a cloudy day, Ramon decided to go **about** / **ahead** / **around** with the picnic.

55 "Put," "take" y "give"

55.1 PHRASAL VERBS CON "PUT"

Liam finished decorating the cake and put it on a stand.

put on
colocar algo sobre una superficie

The deliveryman put the parcel down before knocking on the door.

put down
colocar en el suelo o sobre una superficie algo que llevabas

Angela is upset about her divorce, but she's trying to put it behind her.

put behind
olvidar una mala experiencia

Can you please be quiet? You're putting me off!

put off
no dejar que alguien se concentre

The fitness instructor put the class through a tough training program.

put through
hacer que alguien experimente algo

Forecasters have put out a weather warning for heavy rain and strong winds.

put out
emitir información importante

Cassie followed the instructions carefully to put her new wardrobe together.

put together
construir, montar

Scarlett had to put up with busy trains every day on her way to work.

put up with
tolerar algo desagradable

🔊

55.3 PHRASAL VERBS CON "GIVE"

Martha played the violin as a child, but gave it up when she left school.

give up
dejar de hacer algo

The café on the high street is giving out free samples of their new cakes.

give out
dar gratis algo a alguien

Ver también: give away **51**   give up **26**   put off **23**   put on **6**, **27**, **41**
put through **38**   take away **25**, **30**   take back **10**, **16**, **44**
take in **6**, **51**   take off **5**, **6**, **9**, **22**   take up **15**, **31**

55.2 PHRASAL VERBS CON "TAKE"

Jim's mother asked him to take his younger brother along to the skate park.

take along (to)
llevar a alguien o algo contigo

Amara took her mother aside to tell her that she was pregnant.

take aside
llevar a alguien a un sitio más tranquilo para decirle algo a solas

The waste collectors came to take away the bags of trash.

take away
retirar, llevarse algo

Denise took a jar down from the shelf to give her dog a biscuit.

take down (from)
tomar algo de una posición más elevada

Seeing the black clouds, Tim went outside to take the washing in.

take in
entrar algo

The police stopped the criminal and took the stolen money off him.

take off
quitarle algo a alguien

Eliza has really taken to golf. She never thought she'd like it.

take to
empezar a gustar

The elevator took James up to the top floor of the building.

take up (to)
llevar a alguien o algo más arriba

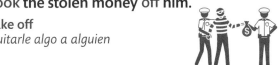
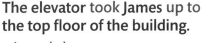

My son had been asking for an ice cream all day. I finally gave in and bought him one.

give in
aceptar hacer algo tras resistirse un poco

Tom's moving to a smaller apartment so he's giving away some of his belongings.

give away
dar gratis algo a alguien (en lugar de venderlo)

Aa 55.4 CONECTA LAS IMÁGENES CON LAS FRASES CORRECTAS

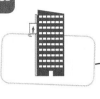

The police stopped the criminal, and took the stolen money off him.

❶

The elevator took James up to the top floor of the building.

❷

Martha played the violin as a child, but gave it up when she left school.

❸

Cassie followed the instructions carefully to put her new wardrobe together.

❹

Liam finished decorating the cake and put it on a stand.

❺

The waste collectors came to take away the bags of trash.

Aa 55.5 TACHA LAS PALABRAS INCORRECTAS DE CADA FRASE

Tom's moving to a smaller apartment so he's giving **away** / ~~over~~ / ~~through~~ some of his belongings.

❶ The café on the high street is **taking** / **putting** / **giving** out samples of their new range of cookies.

❷ Denise **got** / **took** / **put** a jar down from the shelf to give her dog a biscuit.

❸ Angela is upset about her divorce, but she's trying to **put** / **take** / **give** it behind her.

❹ Seeing the black clouds, Tim went outside to take the washing **on** / **off** / **in**.

❺ My son had been asking for an ice cream all day. I finally **took** / **gave** / **put** in and bought him one.

Aa 55.6 CONECTA LOS PRINCIPIOS DE LAS FRASES CON LOS FINALES CORRECTOS

The deliveryman put the parcel — down before knocking on the door.

out free samples of their new cakes.

busy trains every day on her way to work.

1 The fitness instructor put the class

2 Scarlett had to put up with

3 Angela is upset about her divorce,

4 Amara took her mother aside

5 The café on the high street is giving

6 Eliza has really taken to golf.

7 Jim's mother asked him to take

to tell her that she was pregnant.

She never thought she'd like it.

his younger brother along to the skate park.

but she's trying to put it behind her.

through a tough training program.

55.7 ESCUCHA EL AUDIO Y ESCRIBE LAS FRASES BAJO LAS IMÁGENES

Can you please be quiet?
You're putting me off!

1 _____

2 _____

3 _____

4 _____

5 _____

Ver también:
come in **4**   come on **27**, **52**   get out **9**, **53**
go ahead **54**   go away **54**

56.1 EXCLAMACIONES

Go away!

go away
*decirle a alguien o a algo
que te deje solo*

Come on!

come on
*decirle a alguien o a algo que
te siga o vaya más rápido*

Get out!

get out
*decirle a alguien de mala manera
que salga de una habitación*

Look out!

look out
*avisar a alguien de algo de lo
que aún no se ha percatado*

Are you ready to start?   **Yes, bring it on!**

bring it on
*se dice cuando te dispones a
hacer algo con gran confianza*

Hey Vi, can I ask you something?

Sure, fire away.

fire away
*hacer que alguien sepa que
puede empezar a hablar*

I think I've just won the lottery!

Come off it!

come off it
*se dice para expresar incredulidad
ante algo que ha dicho alguien*

Hi Carolina! Come in.

come in
*se dice para invitar a alguien a
entrar en una habitación o un edificio
(especialmente en tu propia casa)*

Do you mind if I sit here?   **Go ahead.**

go ahead
*se dice para dar permiso a alguien
para hacer algo*

56.2 ESCUCHA EL AUDIO Y CONECTA LAS IMÁGENES CON LOS PHRASAL VERBS CORRECTOS

come in

get out

fire away

go ahead

bring it on

Aa 56.3 ESCRIBE EL PHRASAL VERB CORRECTO AL LADO DE SU DEFINICIÓN

se dice para expresar incredulidad ante algo que ha dicho alguien = _come off it_

1 decirle a alguien o a algo que te deje solo = _____

2 avisar a alguien de algo de lo que aún no se ha percatado = _____

3 se dice para dar permiso a alguien para hacer algo = _____

4 hacer que alguien sepa que puede empezar a hablar = _____

5 se dice cuando te dispones a hacer algo con gran confianza = _____

6 decirle a alguien de mala manera que salga de una habitación = _____

7 decirle a alguien o a algo que te siga o vaya más rápido = _____

8 se dice para invitar a alguien a entrar en una habitación o un edificio = _____

go ahead   come on   look out   come in   go away

get out   come off it   bring it on   fire away

229

R1 VERBOS Y PARTÍCULAS

Los verbos pueden ir seguidos de diferentes partículas o preposiciones que cambian su significado. En todas estas frases, "break" da un sentido de separación o daño, pero su significado cambia gracias a las partículas.

Maria and Pablo broke up.
María y Pablo han acabado su relación.

My car broke down.
Mi coche ha dejado de funcionar.

The handle broke off the vase.
El asa se ha separado del jarrón.

Ted broke down and started to cry.
Ted se puso muy sensible y empezó a llorar.

A thief broke into my house.
Un ladrón entró ilegalmente en mi casa.

Gustav broke out of prison.
Gustav se ha fugado de la cárcel.

"Break into" y "break out of" tienen significados opuestos.

R2 PARTÍCULAS HABITUALES

Las partículas de los phrasal verbs suelen dar significados
similares, independientemente del verbo al que acompañen.

PHRASAL VERBS CON "UP"

La partícula "up" suele dar al phrasal verb un significado
de movimiento hacia arriba o aumento.

Try to pay your bills as soon as they arrive. They can soon add up.
acumular

The monkey climbed up the tree with Kazuo's camera.
desplazarse hacia la parte superior de algo

UP

The train left the station slowly before speeding up.
ir más rápido

Sadie's anger about her boss's rude behavior had been building up.
aumentar o reforzarse

Clive lifted his daughter up so that she could see the deer.
levantar a alguien o algo

PHRASAL VERBS CON "DOWN"

La partícula "down" suele dar al phrasal verb un significado
de movimiento hacia abajo, reducción o acción que acaba.

All of the banks in our town have closed down.
cerrar de manera permanente

You should always slow down when you drive past a school.
ir más lento

Your essay's too long, Marcel. You need to cut it down a bit.
reducir en tamaño

DOWN

Joanna is winding down her business to take another job.
cerrar de manera gradual

Rob and I sat on the beach watching the sun go down.
pasar de una posición más elevada a otra más baja

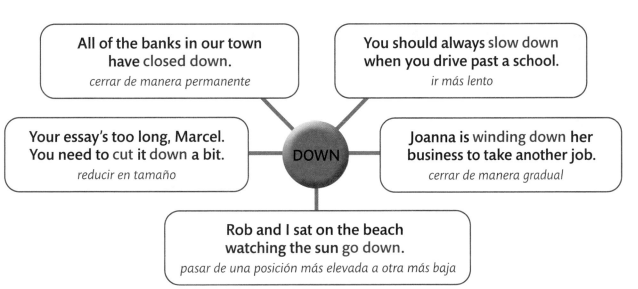

PHRASAL VERBS CON "IN"

La partícula "in" suele dar al phrasal verb un significado de entrar o pasar a formar parte de algo.

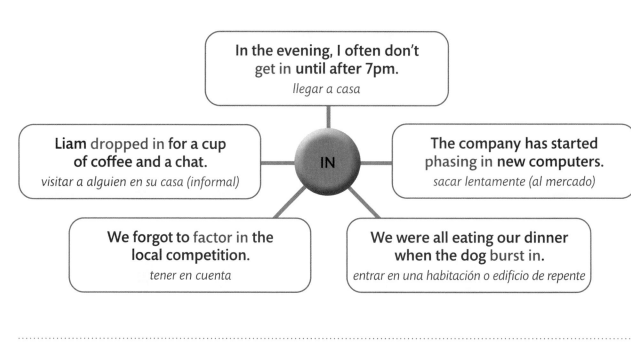

In the evening, I often don't get in until after 7pm.
llegar a casa

Liam dropped in for a cup of coffee and a chat.
visitar a alguien en su casa (informal)

The company has started phasing in new computers.
sacar lentamente (al mercado)

We forgot to factor in the local competition.
tener en cuenta

We were all eating our dinner when the dog burst in.
entrar en una habitación o edificio de repente

IN

PHRASAL VERBS CON "OUT"

La partícula "out" suele dar al phrasal verb un significado de irse o salir.

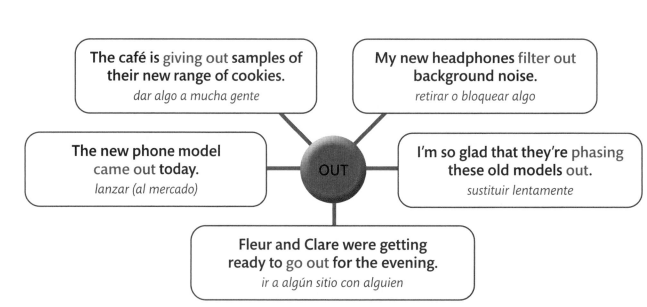

The café is giving out samples of their new range of cookies.
dar algo a mucha gente

My new headphones filter out background noise.
retirar o bloquear algo

The new phone model came out today.
lanzar (al mercado)

I'm so glad that they're phasing these old models out.
sustituir lentamente

Fleur and Clare were getting ready to go out for the evening.
ir a algún sitio con alguien

OUT

PHRASAL VERBS CON "ON"

La partícula "on" suele dar al phrasal verb un significado de continuación o de estar físicamente sobre algo.

Did you leave the lights on when you left the house?
dejar encendido

Can you hang on a minute while I grab my umbrella?
esperar poco tiempo (informal)

The fitting rooms are over there if you'd like to try the dress on.
ponerse una prenda para ver cómo queda

ON

The journey dragged on for hours. The kids were so bored!
continuar durante mucho tiempo (negativo)

George and Yolanda got on the train to Paris.
subir (transporte público)

PHRASAL VERBS CON "BACK"

La partícula "back" suele dar al phrasal verb un significado de volver o hacer algo de nuevo.

The mugs I bought online are broken. I'm going to send them back.
devolver por correo un artículo al vendedor

We brought you back some local olives. They're delicious!
volver con

BACK

I lent Jenny $20 yesterday and she paid me back today.
devolver dinero que te han dejado

I love receiving letters from my dad. I always write back immediately.
responder por carta o correo electrónico

By the time we got back, it was already getting dark.
volver

R3 PHRASAL VERBS SEPARABLES HABITUALES

En algunos casos, el phrasal verb puede ir separado del verbo por el complemento (ver p. 14): primero el verbo, seguido del complemento y, finalmente, la partícula. A menudo esta separación es opcional, salvo si el complemento de un phrasal verb separable es un pronombre, que tiene que ir siempre entre el verbo y la partícula.

PHRASAL VERB	DEFINICIÓN	FRASE DE EJEMPLO
bring around	convencer a alguien para que apoye tu idea	Al's speech **brought** many people **around** to her ideas.
call off	cancelar un acontecimiento	Our manager was busy, so she **called** our meeting **off**.
chop up	cortar en partes pequeñas	**Chop** the onions **up** and then fry them for 10 minutes.
clean up	volver a dejar todo en orden	Can you help me **clean** the kitchen **up** please?
cross out	tachar una palabra	I **crossed out** the wrong word and wrote the right one.
give away	dar gratis algo a alguien	Tom is **giving** some of his furniture **away**.
give up	dejar de hacer algo	Martha used to play the violin, but she **gave** it **up**.
hand out	distribuir	The teacher **handed** some worksheets **out**.
leave out	excluir, no incluir	To make this recipe vegetarian, **leave** the meat **out**.
let in	dejar entrar	I **let** the cat **in** when it started to rain.
let out	dejar salir	I **let** the cat **out** every morning after I've woken up.
make up	inventarse una historia para explicar algo	I don't believe Gio's story, I think he **made** it **up**.
miss out	olvidarse de incluir a alguien o algo	I thought I'd counted everyone, but I **missed** you **out**.
push back	posponer	Claude is unwell, so needs to **push** our meeting **back**.
put back	devolver un objeto a su sitio original	Paul and Sally **put** their furniture **back** in its place.
put in	colocar dentro	Lisa **puts** her rabbit **in** its cage each evening.
put on	colocar algo sobre una superficie	Liam **put** the cake **on** a stand.
take out	llevar a alguien a una cita	Phil **took** me **out** to an expensive restaurant.
take out on	portarse mal con alguien	Stop **taking** it **out on** me. It's not my fault!
throw away	desechar, poner en la basura	If the chicken smells bad, you should **throw** it **away**.
throw on	ponerse una prenda rápidamente	Tom **threw** a jacket **on** and ran for the bus.
try out	probar un producto nuevo para ver qué tal	Marta couldn't wait to **try** her new games console **out**.
turn on	hacer que algo funcione	If you're bored, **turn** the television **on**.
write down	registrar información escribiéndola	I **wrote** a few ideas **down** before starting my essay.

R4 PHRASAL VERBS INSEPARABLES HABITUALES

Algunos phrasal verbs no se pueden separar (ver p. 15) y el complemento
siempre va al final, independientemente de si es un pronombre o no.

PHRASAL VERB	DEFINICIÓN	FRASE DE EJEMPLO
carry on	continuar haciendo algo	The children **carried on** misbehaving.
catch up with	hablar con amigos después de un tiempo	I **caught up with** some friends yesterday.
come across	dar con algo por casualidad	I **came across** some old photographs while cleaning up.
cut back on	gastar menos dinero	The government wants to **cut back on** spending.
deal with	gestionar o solucionar un problema	We learned how to **deal with** difficult customers.
get at	implicar, intentar decir algo de manera indirecta	Sorry, I'm not sure what you're **getting at**.
get off	bajar (transporte público)	George and Yolanda **got on** the train to Paris.
get on	subir (transporte público)	Gine **got off** the bus when it arrived at her stop.
get on with	concentrarse en hacer algo	I need to get on with my homework.
get out of	bajar (de un coche o un taxi)	Be careful when you **get out of** the car.
get over	recuperarse, volver a sentirse bien	It took me a long time to **get over** the last cold I had.
go over	revisar	Remember to **go over** your answers carefully.
go with	conjuntar con otra prenda	Does this scarf **go with** my jacket?
hear from	saber algo de	Have you **heard from** your cousins recently?
keep up with	correr a la misma velocidad	Slow down! I can't **keep up with** you!
live up to	ser tan bueno como esperaban los otros	The movie really **lived up to** everyone's expectations.
look after	cuidar, hacerse responsable de	My mother **looks after** my children when I'm at work.
look for	buscar algo	Peter is going to **look for** a job when he leaves school.
look forward to	esperar algo con muchas ganas	George was **looking forward to** going to the beach.
look up to	admirar a alguien	Lots of young people **look up to** sports stars.
pull through	sobrevivir a una enfermedad u operación grave	It was a risky operation, but Josh **pulled through**.
run out of	no quedar más de algo	We've **run out of** food. Let's go to the store.
turn up	hallar (normalmente por accidente)	I lost my passport, but I'm sure it'll **turn up** soon.
weigh in on	añadir tu opinión a un debate en curso	The professor **weighed in on** the political debate.

R5 SUSTANTIVOS FRASALES HABITUALES

Algunos nombres tienen su origen en phrasal verbs (ver p. 16). A menudo
se combinan en una única palabra o forman un compuesto con un guion.

SUSTANTIVO FRASAL	DEFINICIÓN	FRASE DE EJEMPLO
breakdown	cuando algo (p. ej., un vehículo) deja de funcionar	A **breakdown** on the highway caused heavy traffic.
break-in	acción de entrar en un edificio de manera ilegal	There's been a **break-in** at the local bank.
breakup	final de una relación afectiva	After their **breakup**, John and Helen stayed friends.
checkout	lugar de una tienda donde se paga	Jenny went to the **checkout** to pay for her groceries.
checkup	evaluación (especialmente de salud)	Terry went to the dentist for a **checkup**.
cover-up	acto de ocultar información a alguien	A newspaper exposed the company's **cover-up**.
crackdown	acto de hacer cumplir la ley al pie de la letra	There's been a **crackdown** on littering in the town.
falling-out	discusión o disputa	Idris and Giovanni had a **falling-out**.
getaway	vacaciones	Ellen and Piers went to Mexico for a short **getaway**.
get-together	encuentro social	I'm having a **get-together** for my 30th birthday.
giveaway	acto en el que se distribuyen artículos gratis	The bakery did a **giveaway** to attract more customers.
go-ahead	permiso para hacer algo	My manager gave me the **go-ahead** to leave early.
input	aporte de información u opinión	I asked for my teacher's **input** on my essay.
intake	cantidad de algo que se ingiere	You should limit your daily **intake** of sugar.
kickoff	saque inicial de un partido (p. ej., de fútbol)	Liverpool are playing soccer tonight. **Kickoff**'s at 7pm.
letdown	decepción	I thought I'd like that movie, but it was a real **letdown**.
mix-up	cuando se confunde una cosa con otra	This isn't what I ordered. There's been a **mix-up**.
outset	principio	Harry has worked hard from the **outset**.
printout	copia física de un documento electrónico	Jim gave everyone a **printout** of the presentation.
setback	obstáculo o retraso	There were a lot of **setbacks** during the project.
sleepover	cuando duermes en casa de otro	Phoebe went for a **sleepover** at Eliza's house.
stopover	parada de camino hacia otro sitio	Our flight to Los Angeles had a **stopover** in New York.
takeout (US) / takeaway (UK)	comida que compras y te llevas para comértela (especialmente en casa)	I don't want to cook. Let's order some **takeout** instead.
workout	período de ejercicio	Dimitri was exhausted after his **workout**.

R6 ADJETIVOS FRASALES HABITUALES

Algunos adjetivos tienen su origen en phrasal verbs (ver p. 17). A menudo se combinan en una única palabra o forman un compuesto con un guion.

ADJETIVO FRASAL	DEFINICIÓN	FRASE DE EJEMPLO
backup	apoyo o alternativa	I always make a **backup** copy of all my files.
beaten-up	viejo y en mal estado	Ken's finally getting rid of his old, **beaten-up** car.
broken-down	(normalmente un vehículo) que ya no funciona	A **broken-down** truck caused delays on the highway.
bygone	del pasado lejano	These old photographs are from a **bygone** era.
drawn-out	que dura mucho tiempo (negativo)	Buying a house can be a stressful, **drawn-out** process.
follow-up	de seguimiento	My doctor and I scheduled a **follow-up** appointment.
getaway	usado para huir	The thieves escaped in a **getaway** car.
incoming	que llega	Everyone rushed to prepare for the **incoming** storm.
knockdown	más bajo que de costumbre o que antes	Kemal sold some of his jewelry at a **knockdown** price.
leftover	lo que queda tras utilizar el resto	There's some **leftover** chicken in the fridge.
made-up	inventado, no real	Wayne is always telling his friends **made-up** stories.
off-putting	desaliñado, poco atractivo	I found the violence in the movie very **off-putting**.
ongoing	en progreso	There's an **ongoing** investigation into their finances.
outdated	anticuado, pasado de moda	I'm replacing my **outdated** computer with a new one.
outgoing	sociable, extrovertido	Kerry is a very friendly and **outgoing** person.
outspoken	obstinado, que da su opinión	My dad is very **outspoken** about environmental issues.
outstanding	excelente	Chris's professor told him his essay was **outstanding**.
outstretched	estirado al máximo	Finn approached me with his arms **outstretched**.
run-down	en malas condiciones	Paolo is renovating an old, **run-down** house.
stressed-out	ansioso por algo	Somrita is **stressed-out** with work at the moment.
tired out	extenuado	Vi is feeling **tired out** after a long day at work.
upcoming	que tiene lugar en el futuro inmediato	The country is preparing for the **upcoming** election.
uplifting	inspirador, alentador	Jo was feeling sad, so she watched an **uplifting** movie.
worn-out	extenuado, absolutamente cansado	Gerry was completely **worn-out** after his run.

Respuestas

01

1.3
1. La gente salió en masa del estadio.
2. Le ha adulado para obtener un favor.
3. Creen que ellos son mejores que ella.
4. Encontré el retrato por casualidad.

1.4
1. Jordan's aunts fuss over him when they visit.
2. I found it hard to fit in with the art class.
3. Nuwa gathered up the plates from the table.
4. Sandra was asking after you at the park.

1.5
1. Some of the older children have been **ganging** up on me and calling me names.
2. Ava lost her passport ages ago It turned **up** when she was cleaning the living room.
3. Adi has got a temper. He **turned** on me the instant I suggested he buy a new suit.
4. Mel lent Dave her lawnmower a month ago, and she finally got it **back** from him.

1.6
1. turn up 2. watch over 3. turn on
4. wear down 5. pack into

1.7
1. Some of the older children have been **ganging up** on me and calling me names.
2. Mel lent Dave her lawnmower a month ago, and she finally **got** it **back** from him.
3. I got my son a puppy. After asking me for months, he finally **wore** me **down**!
4. Hundreds of people **packed into** the town hall to watch the debate.
5. Barney really **looks up to** his grandfather. He loves listening to his stories.

02

2.3
1. I let the cat in when it started to rain.
2. Olly's dog ran away last week while they were at the park.
3. My mother looks after my children while I'm at work.

2.4
1. After a few days, Olly's dog came back all by herself.
2. Jasmine takes after her mother. They're very similar people.
3. I let the cat out every morning after I've woken up.
4. Albert's parents named him after his great-grandfather.
5. After traveling for a few years, Bill settled down and bought a house.
6. Colin lives with his son in a house at the edge of town.

2.5
1. Lisa puts her rabbit **in** its cage each evening before bed.
2. Will and Joe are identical twins. It's almost impossible to tell them **apart**.
3. After traveling for a few years, Bill settled **down** and bought a house next door to his parents.
4. Liam gets **on** very well with his elder sister. They're always laughing together.
5. Fiona's cat doesn't like strangers, but he's warming **to** Dan.
6. Jenny's grown **out** of her old toys, she prefers playing video games now.

2.6
1. Will and Joe are identical twins. It's almost impossible to **tell** them **apart**.
2. Lisa **puts** her rabbit **in** its cage each evening before bed.
3. Jasmine **takes after** her mother. They're very similar people.
4. I **let** the cat **out** every morning after I've woken up.
5. Jenny's **grown out of** her old toys, she prefers playing video games now.

03

3.3
Ⓐ 3 Ⓑ 2 Ⓒ 1 Ⓓ 5 Ⓔ 4 Ⓕ 6

3.4
1. My brother **set me up** with a woman who works at his office.
2. Jack and Ula **really care for** each other. They've been together for 50 years.
3. They started **going out with** each other when they were at school.
4. Misha **stood by Colin** when he decided to quit college.

3.5
1. go off 2. bring together 3. fizzle out
4. set up 5. drift apart 6. finish with
7. care for

3.6
1. My best friends and I have **stuck together** since high school.
2. For our first date, Phil **took** me **out** to an expensive restaurant.
3. Bernadette **confided in** Martha that she was in love with Pavel.
4. Luisa has **finished with** Ben. He's very upset.
5. Ken **stuck by** Cath when her restaurant went bankrupt.

04

4.3
1. show around 2. invite along 3. show out 4. snoop around 5. stay over

4.4
1. Ha llegado a las 6.
2. Me enseñaron su casa.
3. Llevaron a los niños con ellos.
4. Nos gustaría que vinieras a casa.
5. Pasó por casa a visitarme.

4.5
1. On her way home from the gym, **Miriam stopped off at the supermarket.**
2. My father came into the house **and took off his coat.**
3. Omar told us to come over **any time after 2pm.**
4. After chatting on the doorstep, **Malik invited me in.**
5. We ended up staying over **at Beth and Omar's** house.
6. While everyone was in the garden, **I found Klaus snooping around inside.**

4.6
1. My new neighbors, Kaito and Leiko, **had** me **over** for dinner last night.
2. We chatted for hours, and he suggested I **stick around** for dinner.
3. On our way home from the beach, we **called in** to see Grandma.
4. Omar told us to **come over** any time after 2pm.
5. While you're in town, try to **swing by**. It would be good to see you.

05

5.3

1 Amara let her little sister tag **along** when she went to the ice rink.

2 Ella likes to get **together** with her friends at the ice cream parlor.

3 I hate to tear you **away**, but we're going to miss the last train.

4 Katie asked Lisa if she wanted to come **out** to play.

5 Joe suddenly took **off** without saying where he was going.

5.4

1 Charlie stormed **out of** the store when the manager refused to give him a refund.

2 As I was leaving for the art exhibition, I asked Joe if he wanted to come **along**.

3 Lots of guests were milling **around**, waiting for Raj to make his speech.

4 Vincent and Maya decided to stay **in**. They ordered pizza and watched a movie.

5 We headed **off to** the beach early because we wanted to avoid the crowds.

6 Once a year, my school friends and I go out for a meal together to catch **up**.

5.5

1 shoot off
2 mill around
3 liven up
4 stay out

5.6

1 Nadiya had to **dash off to pick** up the kids from school.

2 The carnival was amazing. **We stayed out until** dawn.

3 Fleur and Clare were getting **ready to go out** for the evening.

4 Our local hotel has a large room that **it hires out for** parties.

06

6.2

1 All the children at the party had dressed up as dinosaurs.

2 Maurice hung up his coat as he walked in.

3 Angelica helped her son to button up his shirt as he got ready for school.

4 I hope this juice stain comes out when I wash my shirt.

6.3

1 Marlon zipped up his leather jacket and walked toward the door.

2 Gemma's shoes go really well with that dress.

3 Arnie's so proud of his new jacket. He's been showing it off to everyone.

4 Zane folded up his clothes and put them in the wardrobe.

6.4

A 3 **B** 6 **C** 1 **D** 4 **E** 7 **F** 2 **G** 5

6.5

1 Mirek **did up** his coat to keep out the icy breeze.

2 Kelly stopped to **tie up** one of her shoe laces.

3 The sun is really strong today, so make sure you **cover up**.

4 Gio's **grown out of** his sweater, so he's going to give it to his little brother.

5 Alex **put on** her prettiest dress to go out for her wedding anniversary.

07

7.3

1 Heavy traffic has had a strong effect on the city's air quality.

2 Old cell phones aren't as good as today's smartphones.

3 Due to her injury, Colleen had to accept the fact that she couldn't play in the match.

4 To get into college, you'll need to get better results than you got last year.

7.4

1 Sanjay got 100% on his exam. He more than **measured up to** his parents' expectations.

2 The new action movie really **lived up to** the crowd's expectations.

3 The discovery of some ancient ruins has **led to** an increase in tourism.

4 The invention of the computer **brought about** the end of the typewriter.

5 The heavy rain **resulted in** floods throughout the city.

08

8.5

1 no despertarse al sonar el despertador
2 irse a la cama
3 quedarse despierto
4 tumbarse
5 hacer tareas sencillas de forma relajada
6 asearse
7 salir de la cama

8.6

1 sleep over **2** sleep in
3 get in **4** get up
5 go off

8.7

1 wake up
2 head off (to)
3 doze off
4 sit down
5 set about

8.8

1 After a short break, Ramone **got on with** cleaning the bathroom.

2 Martina **stayed up late** studying for her exam the following morning.

3 I tried to wake Mia when I saw she had **dozed off at** her desk.

4 Quite a few people **nodded off during** the speech.

09

9.3

1 I got lost driving to your house. I had to pull over and ask for directions.

2 Tanya turned off the main road and drove along the track to the beach.

3 The helicopter took off from the top of the skyscraper.

4 Gina got off the bus when it arrived at her stop.

5 The train left the station slowly, before speeding up as it headed to the coast.

9.4

1 Jen turned **back** when she realized that she had forgotten her phone.

2 I pulled **up** by the train station to let my daughter out.

3 Sally picked her friends **up** outside the movie theater at 9pm.

4 When you reach the castle, turn **onto** the highway and head west.

5 Jamie dropped me **off** at the train station on his way to work.

6 Angelo left his house and got **into** the taxi.

7 Marion didn't notice the motorcycle as she pulled **out of** the junction.

239

9.5

1. As the movie star **got out of** the limousine, photographers surrounded him.
2. We **pulled in** at a small roadside café, where we could have some breakfast.
3. The plane **touched down** in Dubai at 9pm in the evening.
4. You should always **slow down** when you drive past a school.
5. Clive tried to restart the motorboat's engine after it **cut out** without any warning.

9.6

1. get on   2. slow down   3. break down
4. drive off   5. turn onto

10

10.2

1. The fitting rooms are over there if you'd like to wear the clothes to see if they fit.
2. The mugs I bought online are broken. I'm going to return them to the seller by mail.
3. I bought my new laptop online, and went to collect it from my local store.
4. Before buying a new car, it's worth visiting several stores to compare prices.
5. I went to the market to buy some bread, but all the bread had been sold.

10.3

1. line up   2. stock up (on)   3. cross off
4. sell out (of)   5. snap up

10.4

1. Marta couldn't wait to **try out** her new games console.
2. Kemal **knocked down** the price of jewelry by 15% to attract shoppers to his new store.
3. Luis put the melon in his basket and **checked it off** his shopping list.
4. Aisha decided to **splash out on** clothes for her summer vacation.
5. Ellie used her credit card to **pay for** the scarf.

10.5

1. Aziz had been looking **around** the store for ages, but couldn't find a shirt he liked.
2. Shoppers had already snapped **up** all the bargains at the sale by the time I'd arrived.
3. Once Ellie had found a scarf that she liked, she went to check **out**.
4. Carla didn't like the sweater she'd bought, so she decided to take it **back**.
5. Joshua crossed **off** each item on the shopping list as he found it.

11

11.2

1. Today started off nicely, so we ate our breakfast on the terrace.
2. After days of bad weather, the rain finally started to let up.
3. Chris and Mel had to leave the beach when it started bucketing down.
4. The weather's been awful, but it's finally starting to brighten up.

11.3

1. Minutes after Ben had lit the grill, the sky clouded over.
2. People go ice-skating when the lake freezes over in the winter.
3. The wind's picking up. It's perfect weather for flying a kite.
4. Alice likes to sit on the balcony when the weather cools down in the evening.

11.4

1. As soon as the storm had **blown over,** the hikers left the cave and continued walking.
2. As dark storm clouds **rolled in** from the east, Arthur tried to get home before the rain started.
3. It looks like the weather's **clearing up**. We'll be able to start the game again soon.
4. By the end of May, the weather starts to **warm up** and the tourists start to arrive.
5. Once the storm had **calmed down,** Grace checked her house for damage.

11.5

A 4   B 1   C 7   D 2   E 6   F 3   G 8   H 5

12

12.4

A 5   B 1   C 7   D 4   E 2   F 6   G 3

12.5

1. When Amy zoomed in, she noticed the red car in front of the restaurant.
2. Some criminals hacked into our computer system and stole the new designs.
3. Pete scrolled up to the top of the document to find the company's address.

12.6

1. You should **shut down** your computer at night to save electricity.

2. **Click on** the link at the bottom of the page to see the answers.
3. I **back up** all my photos in case my computer breaks.
4. Always make sure you **log out** of your account after using it.
5. The company has started **phasing in** new computers. They look great!

12.7

1. I **type out** my essays because it's quicker than writing them by hand.
2. I **printed out** a copy of the contract for the clients to sign.
3. Our company hired a technician to **set up** the new printer.
4. You have to **type in** your password to access the website.
5. Amy **zoomed out** to look at the whole picture at once.

13

13.3

1. One of my old school friends is a candidate for mayor.
2. The police stopped people from entering the area where the crime had taken place.
3. After robbing the store, the thieves escaped in a stolen car.
4. Be aware of pickpockets when you're on the train!
5. The police are becoming stricter on illegal parking in the city.
6. Activists are asking the government publicly to protect the country's forests.

13.4

A 7   B 1   C 4   D 2   E 6   F 3   G 5   H 8

13.5

1. The police ordered the criminal to hand over the stolen money.
2. Senators voted on the new law after a long debate.
3. Janice is leading a campaign to stamp out littering in the park.
4. While I was driving home, the traffic police pulled me over for speeding.
5. Dan tipped off the police about the location of the stolen artworks.

13.6

1. vote for   2. turn to   3. track down
4. beat up   5. bring in   6. call for

14

14.2
1. La empresa ha perdido valor.
2. Tommy gastó mucho dinero.
3. Heredé mucho dinero.
4. Patrick ingresó dinero en el banco.
5. Pagamos a Wayne lo que le debíamos.

14.3
1. pay up 2. wipe off 3. run up
4. chip in 5. live on
6. save up

14.4
1. Sara has finally **coughed up** the money I lent her last year.
2. I've decided to **cut back on** spending by bringing my own lunch to work.
3. The food was excellent, but we were shocked when the bill **came to** more than $200.
4. The cost of the new stadium has already **run into** the millions.
5. Try to pay your bills as soon as they arrive. They can soon **add up**.

14.5
1. The cost of the new stadium has already run into the millions.
2. The food was excellent, but we were shocked when the bill came to more than $200.
3. Tara and Ali are saving up for a new house. They try to save $300 each month.
4. Tommy had to fork out more than $600 to get his car repaired.
5. Pete went to the ATM to take out some cash.

15

15.3
1. Apresúrate, Oliver.
2. Tengo más tiempo para estudiar.
3. Empecé a querer a Phil.
4. Sus lecciones son muy largas.
5. Me gustar pasar el rato leyendo.
6. Se le ha acabado el tiempo.
7. Tu sesión ha finalizado por falta de actividad.

15.4
1. drag out 2. hurry up 3. wait for
4. break up 5. while away

15.5
1. The journey **dragged on** for hours. The kids were so bored.
2. Commuting to and from work really **eats into** my time.
3. Cleaning the house **took up** all of Liam's weekend.
4. The deadline for the project **crept up on** us.

15.6
1. The service here is terrible! It's **holding everyone up**.
2. Time's **getting on now**. Let's hurry home before it gets dark.
3. Can you **hang on a** minute while I grab my umbrella?
4. The doctor's busy today, but I'll try to **fit you in** tomorrow.

16

16.4
A 6 B 1 C 4 D 2 E 7 F 5 G 3 H 8

16.5
1. In my country, the clocks go **forward** by one hour in the spring.
2. The clocks go **back** by one hour in the fall.
3. Elly and George are looking **forward to** going to the beach later.
4. Claude is unwell today We'll have to push our meeting back **to** tomorrow.
5. Finding my old toys brought **back** happy memories of my childhood.
6. The building project has just begun Months of construction work lie **ahead**.
7. We are planning to turn the store back **into** a house and live there.
8. All the streets were decorated in the weeks leading **up** to the festival.

16.6
1. This dress takes me back to **my childhood in the 1960s**.
2. Kira had dreamed of becoming a great actor, **but her plans didn't pan out**.
3. Peter reminds me of you **when you were a little boy**.
4. Many of the buildings in my city **date back to the 19th century**.
5. The house was turned into **a convenience store in the 1980s**.

16.7
1. The doctor's off tomorrow, so could we **bring** your appointment **forward to** today?
2. Colin is working hard because the deadline for his article is **coming up**.
3. Roland **looks back on** his college days with pleasure.
4. All the streets were decorated in the weeks **leading up to** the festival.
5. I like to listen to music and **think back to** my days as a musician in Paris.
6. The building project has just begun. Months of construction work **lie ahead**.

17

17.3
1. Take traffic delays into consideration when estimating how long the journey will take.
2. We've been meaning to get a new kitchen for years, but haven't found the time for it.
3. Giovanni forgot about the art project, but he managed to do it without preparation.
4. The two directors had several meetings to make the new contract more definite.
5. I asked Sabrina if she wanted to go camping, but she rejected the idea.
6. The negotiating teams stayed up to discuss and reach an agreement on a new treaty.

17.4
1. They stayed up until after midnight **hammering out** a new treaty.
2. Cleo pretended to be sick to **get out of** going out.
3. Dexter was going to ask Becky out, but he **chickened out**.
4. You need to **think ahead** and save money for the future.

17.5
1. You should **plan ahead** before setting off on a long car journey.
2. Seb said he'd help me paint the house, but he **went back on** his promise.
3. **Look ahead** and picture what you want to be doing in five years' time.
4. The store **weaseled out of** giving us a refund by claiming we had broken the vase.
5. Ed had promised to do a bungee jump with me, but **backed out** at the last minute.

17.6
A 6 B 5 C 1 D 3 E 2 F 7 G 4

18.4

1. La sopa sabe a tomate y albahaca.
2. Marcus ha utilizado su telescopio.
3. Robert buscaba sus gafas.
4. ¡Escúchame!

18.5

1. stink out
2. look at
3. listen out for
4. listen in on
5. sniff around
6. look through

18.6

1. sniff around 2. look at 3. look out over
4. look away

18.7

1. listen in (on)
2. stink out
3. look out for
4. hear about
5. listen up
6. hear out
7. look on

18.8

1. Alex's cookies **smelled of** cinnamon. I asked to try one.
2. Have you **heard about** the new gym in town? It's supposed to be great.
3. Dayita **listened to** the radio while she ate her breakfast.
4. Fiona **spied on** her colleagues to steal their ideas.
5. Sarah and Dionne **looked into** the well. There was no sign of the bottom.

19.3

A 2 B 5 C 1 D 3 E 4

19.4

1. Kazuo got the monkey to climb **down by offering it a banana**.
2. The explorers walked **into the cave**.
3. Doug dropped back to help one of **the other hikers, who had injured himself**.
4. As we came down from the summit, **the weather became much worse**.

5. The saleswoman came up **to Fabio and asked if he needed any help**.
6. Clive lifted his daughter up s**o that she could see the deer**.

19.5

1. When I heard someone calling my name, I turned **around**.
2. Martin was exhausted, and began to **fall** behind the other runners.
3. Clive lifted his daughter **up** so that she could see the deer.
4. Janine grabbed her coat and walked **out** of the room.
5. Doug dropped **back** to help one of the other hikers, who had injured himself.

19.6

1. Tanya **turned away as** the nurse gave her the injection.
2. The monkey **climbed up the** tree with Kazuo's camera.
3. Helen told her son to **get down from** the garden wall.
4. As the train **went through the** mountain range, Ted took some photographs.

20.3

1. Leo is the youngest in his class, but manages to keep up with his classmates.
2. She's looking into how astronauts might travel to Mars one day.
3. Sam has dived into his new project. He spent all weekend working on it.
4. The library was full of students swotting up on English grammar.
5. At the start of your presentation, lay out the main points you are going to discuss.

20.4

1. Noah **is majoring in** international politics at college.
2. I kept making mistakes, so I decided **to start over**.
3. Patsy's research **focuses on space** travel.
4. Fiona **worked through the** problems in her code to fix the issues.

20.5

1. work through
2. move on to
3. count toward

4. mark down
5. focus on
6. lay out

20.6

A 5 B 1 C 8 D 3 E 4 F 2 G 7 H 6

21.3

1. Las escuelas cierran en julio.
2. Marco no ha castigado a Gio y Carmen.
3. Zosia riñó a los niños.
4. Rosie responde mal a sus maestros.

21.4

1. After the class, Arun packed up his things and got ready to leave.
2. Miguel handed in his assignment just before the deadline.
3. Ramu's working on a huge painting of New York.
4. The teacher handed out the worksheet to each student.

21.5

1. not stand for 2. hand in 3. drop out
4. play up

21.6

1. hand out (to) 2. wipe off 3. not stand for
4. drop out 5. turn to

21.7

1. Good morning class. Please **take out** your books.
2. The kids have been **playing up** all morning.
3. Despite the teacher's warnings, the children **carried on** misbehaving.
4. You've spent too much time **goofing off** this semester, Jesse.
5. Mateo and Juanita are very naughty, but Martina lets them **get away with** it.

22.4

1. Ted used to be very proactive, but he's been **slacking off** lately.
2. I've got lots to do! I need to **knuckle down** and get it finished.
3. Angela **meets up with** her colleagues once a week to discuss all their new ideas.

4 Our manager was busy, so she had to **call off** our meeting.
5 Jennie's been **slogging away** trying to finish writing her presentation.
6 Kamal's manager **chased up** the report, which was already a week late.
7 I **clock in** at 9am every morning.

22.5
Ⓐ, Ⓒ, Ⓓ, Ⓕ, Ⓖ, Ⓘ

22.6
1 I'm not feeling very well today, so I'm going to call in sick.
2 I've been very busy lately, but I have next week off work.
3 I clock off at 5pm every afternoon.
4 Ola is carrying out a survey about worker satisfaction.

22.7
1 The applications for the new manager position are **piling up**. I'd better start looking through them.
2 Fiona was struggling to finalize the company's accounts, but she kept **plugging away** at them.
3 Debbie **took** the afternoon **off** so she could go to the dentist.
4 Despite the storm, the engineers **soldiered on** and installed the new phone line.

23

23.2
1 go back to
2 draw on
3 head up
4 stick with

23.3
1 Fue fácil para Elliot encontrar empleo.
2 Katie saca partido de su experiencia.
3 Naina planea convertirse en profesora.
4 He vuelto a trabajar.
5 Diana dirige el nuevo departamento.
6 Chad busca empleo en comunicación.
7 Olivia intenta convertirse en periodista.

23.4
1 stick with
2 apply for
3 take over
4 go back to
5 wind down

23.5
1 get into
2 burn out
3 branch out (into)
4 put off
5 cash in on
6 fall back on
7 set out

24

24.2
1 The bank agreed to write off the debt, saving Ethan's company from bankruptcy.
2 We are proud to announce that our two banks are entering into a partnership.
3 Mario's gas station has just gone under. It had been struggling for a long time.
4 Katie's trying to drum up interest in her café by offering free samples of her cakes.

24.3
1 Marco's garden center is doing well. It turns **over** almost $250,000 a year.
2 We need the CEO to **sign** off on this important decision.
3 The board has finally **come** to a decision about the new logo for the company.
4 Ellie's company deals **in** antiques. She sells pieces from all over the world.
5 Could you **draw** up a contract for our new clients?
6 The company is facing difficulties. We may need to lay **off** some staff.

24.4
1 fall through
2 come to
3 sign off
4 drum up
5 enter into
6 profit from

24.5
1 Our business is growing, so we are **taking on** more staff.
2 A new bookstore is **opening up** in our neighborhood.
3 Chrissie has just **started up** her own hair salon. It opened last week.
4 Gemma has **bought out** all the other partners.
5 Al's store is **selling off** a lot of its stock.
6 Alan's sportswear company **profited from** the cold weather.

25

25.3
1 The number of people buying clothes online shot up last year.
2 The coach divided the children up into two equal teams.
3 Shreya counted up the number of people wanting coffee and went to make some.
4 When Georgia was paying her check, she added on a 20% tip.

25.4
Ⓐ 3 Ⓑ 1 Ⓒ 6 Ⓓ 2 Ⓔ 4 Ⓕ 5

25.5
1 Katie's bills have been **stacking up**. She's in a lot of debt now.
2 The company's share price has been falling, but it's finally starting to **bottom out**.
3 The temperature varies a bit in the summer, but it **averages out at** about 25°C.
4 We estimated the cost of the project to be £14,900, but **rounded** it **up to** the nearest thousand.
5 If you want to set yourself a budget, start by **adding up** all your monthly expenses.

25.6
1 count down **2** add up **3** average out (at) **4** level out **5** count out **6** bottom out

26

26.4
1 scrape by **2** carry off **3** win out **4** sail through **5** run into **6** give up **7** screw up

26.5
1 screw up **2** carry off **3** win out **4** come off **5** run into

26.6
1 My teachers told me I'd never amount to anything, but now I'm a lawyer.
2 Anita's hard work has paid off. The dress looks beautiful.
3 Many smaller stores have lost out since the supermarket opened in town.
4 Nia built on her experience working at a hotel to set up her own guesthouse.
5 Having supportive parents really contributed to my success.

26.7

1 Clive **muddled through** the interview without any preparation. He was shocked when he got the job.
2 When I didn't get into college, I started my own successful business. Everything **worked out** in the end!
3 The Scottish team **pulled off** an amazing victory, scoring two goals in the last four minutes.
4 When Al saw how many people were making money by selling things online, he decided to **get in on** it.
5 Kwase **sailed through** his driving test. He didn't make any mistakes.

27

27.4

1 If you're bored, **turn on** the television. There's a good movie on tonight.
2 When Ben got home, he realized that he'd forgotten his keys and was **locked out**.
3 My parents have decided to **move away** and live in the country.
4 When Elsa heard her favorite song on the radio, she **turned up** the volume.
5 The street lights **come on** at dusk, when the sun sets.
6 The lights in the house **went out**, so Clara lit some candles.
7 We finally sold our house. We're **moving out** today.

27.5

1 go off
2 move in
3 lock out
4 turn on
5 turn down

27.6

A 3 B 1 C 6 D 2 E 5 F 4

27.7

1 turn off 2 lock in 3 leave on
4 turn down 5 come on

28

28.3

1 put back 2 chop down 3 pitch in
4 pull up 5 take out 6 clear out
7 wash up

28.4

1 Nousha's room looked much nicer after she'd put **up** some pictures.
2 Paul spent the whole afternoon pulling **up** weeds.
3 Karl swept **up** the trash from the party and put it into bags.
4 After finishing the gardening, Scott put his tools **away**.
5 Jason told me to mop **up** the water that I'd spilled on the floor.

28.5

1 The tree in our backyard died, so we had to **chop it down**.
2 I'm **digging up** the lavender bushes so I can move them to a different part of the garden.
3 I **wipe down** the table each evening after we've eaten.
4 We need to **tidy up** before the guests arrive.
5 The hedge in Doug's yard was getting too big, so he **cut it back**.

28.6

1 On Tuesday mornings, I **take** the trash **out**.
2 If the chicken smells bad, **throw** it **out**.
3 Ian **hung** his washing **out** to dry.
4 We **cleared out** the garage this weekend.
5 There was a mess to **clean up** after the party.

29

29.3

1 I always **cut off** the fat from the meat before cooking it.
2 My breakfast typically **consists of** bread and cheese, served with coffee.
3 Nadiya left the cherry pie on the windowsill to **cool down**.
4 Before serving the curry I made sure to **fish out** any bones.
5 My sister can **whip up** a tasty meal in minutes from just a few ingredients.

29.4

1 chop up
2 set aside
3 cut off
4 mix in
5 pour in
6 finish off
7 fish out
8 cool down
9 leave out

29.5

1 Patrick broke up the chocolate before adding it to the cake mixture.
2 My sister can whip up a tasty meal in minutes from just a few ingredients.
3 The sauce boiled over, leaving a mess on the stove top.
4 I always measure out all of my ingredients before trying a new recipe.
5 We managed to fill up three jars with the cookies we'd baked.

29.6

1 After chopping the vegetables, **set** them **aside**.
2 **Cut off** the fat from the meat before cooking it.
3 When the meat is cooked, **pour in** the stock.
4 **Mix in** the eggs with the other ingredients.
5 **Finish off** the stew by adding chopped parsley.
6 Before serving, make sure to **fish out** any bones.
7 For a vegetarian version, **leave out** the meat.

30

30.3

1 I washed down my pizza **with a cold drink.**
2 Our restaurant can cater for **about 100 customers at a time.**
3 After the wedding, **we all drank to the bride and groom.**
4 Lisa shared out the chocolates, **giving the children two each.**
5 I was going to make a lasagna, **but we've run out of pasta.**

30.4

1 Paul and Sarah ordered two hamburgers and sodas to take **away**.
2 The café was about to close, so we drank **up** and got ready to leave.
3 I washed **down** my pizza with a cold drink.
4 After a long day at the beach, my kids wolfed **down** their dinner.
5 Daniel broke **off** a piece of bread and dipped it in the olive oil.

30.5

1 run out of 2 go off 3 eat up
4 wash down 5 go together

30.6

1 eat out 2 top up 3 drink to 4 eat in
5 go together

31

31.3

1 Ken's currently working **toward** getting a black belt in judo.
2 Nathan told his daughters to stop lazing **about**, and help to tidy the house.
3 After the exam, the students went to the local park to wind **down**.
4 I recently got back **into** cycling. I hadn't done it since I was a teenager.
5 On Friday evenings, Josh likes to kick **back** and watch some television.
6 Anastasia absolutely lives **for** skiing. She goes to the mountains whenever she can.

31.4

1 Adi's painting skills are really coming along. He might become an artist one day.
2 I found running very hard when I started, but I get a lot of satisfaction out of it now.
3 Learning the piano isn't easy, but if you stick at it, you could become a great pianist.
4 Fabio could have been a great guitarist, but he threw it all away by never practicing.

31.5

1 curl up 2 start out 3 sit around
4 live for

31.6

1 I spend most Sundays lying about the house.
2 Aden needs to loosen up and dance with us.
3 On my days off, I like to sit around the garden.
4 Luiza spent the evening curled up on the couch.
5 After a stressful day, I take a bath to chill out.

32

32.2

1 heal up 2 throw up 3 flare up
4 come around 5 seize up 6 go around

32.3

1 Elaine's rash began to clear **up** after she started using the cream.
2 I think I'm coming down **with** the flu.
3 Ella's been throwing **up** all day.
4 My son passed **on** the virus to his sisters.
5 It's taken me weeks to get **over** this cold, but I finally feel better.

32.4

1 Paola's hay fever usually **flares up** in the spring.
2 After a few hours, the swelling had started to **go down**.
3 Danny's thumb **swelled up** after he was stung by a wasp.
4 My brother's a nurse. He **cares for** sick people at the local hospital.
5 I was very sad to hear that your grandmother has **passed away**.

32.5

1 care for 2 feel up to 3 go around
4 wear off 5 pull through

33

33.3

1 After finishing the race, Sandra warmed **down** by stretching her legs.
2 Jamal was completely wiped **out** after cycling up the mountain.
3 Clara was sent **off** the pitch after pushing over another player.
4 Five runners have gotten **through** to the final. Whoever wins this race will win the trophy.
5 My sister is a judo champion She ranks **among** the best in the country.
6 I struggle to keep **up** with my brother. He's much fitter than I am.

33.4

1 Before playing a game of soccer, I always warm up by jogging slowly.
2 For this yoga position, you have to stretch your arms out as far as you can.
3 Pete wanted to start playing baseball, so he signed up for his school team.
4 Angela knocked Kirsten out in the first round of the competition.
5 My knee injury kept me from completing the marathon this year.

33.5

1 Clara was sent off the pitch after pushing over another player.
2 The crowd cheered Tony on as he approached the finish line.
3 I picked up my bow and aimed another arrow at the target.
4 Playing tennis all afternoon with Gus has worn Charlie out.
5 Leo works out at his local gym every morning.

33.6

1 keep up (with) 2 warm up 3 size up
4 turn around 5 burn off 6 cheer on
7 work off

34

34.4

1 The new music channel is **aimed at** people who like jazz.
2 At the start of the horror movie, scary music started to **fade in**.
3 My new headphones help me concentrate by **filtering out** background noise.
4 This new TV show **feeds on** people's curiosity about aliens.
5 The noise from the parade **faded away** as it moved away from us.
6 I **tune into** my favorite radio show every Sunday morning.

34.5

1 This new TV show feeds on people's curiosity about aliens.
2 I tune into my favorite radio show every Sunday morning.
3 The architects have mocked up a model of the new museum.
4 The new music channel is aimed at people who like jazz.
5 Greg and Chloe colored in pictures of dinosaurs after their trip to the museum.

35

35.2

1 get around
2 check in
3 get back from
4 put up
5 soak up

35.3

1 We brought you back some local olives.
2 They checked out of the hotel.
3 Marimar and I went off to Miami recently.
4 It was great to get away for a few days!

35.4

1 On our way to Barcelona, **we stopped over in a hotel for the night**.
2 Whenever we set out on a hike, **we always take a compass and a map**.

3 We set off for Chicago at dawn **when there would be less traffic.**
4 When she arrived at the hotel, **Julia went to the reception to check in.**
5 We managed to put the tent up **even though it was raining heavily.**

35.5
1 When Krishna **arrived at** the villa, the party had begun.
2 We're **packing in** lots of sightseeing during our vacation.
3 It was great to **get away** for a few days.
4 We've been in Cyprus for a few days, but we're **heading for** Athens on today.
5 On your way to London, you'll **pass by** Cambridge.

36

36.2
1 Kirsty talked the workers **through the new software system.**
2 Shona wanted to dye her hair purple, **but her sister talked her out of it.**
3 Diana is always rambling on about **how things were better when she was a child.**
4 Uncle Toby still talks down to me l**ike I'm a child, even though I'm 25.**
5 Shut up **and listen to me for once!**
6 My kids talked me into **getting a puppy.**

36.3
1 drown out
2 mouth off
3 ramble on
4 tone down
5 talk down
6 launch into

36.4
A 6 B 1 C 2
D 4 E 3
F 5

36.5
1 I think you should **tone down** your language.
2 Andy **blurted out** the name of the winner by mistake.
3 The lecturer **droned on** for what felt like hours.
4 Marco is always **talking at** people and not letting them speak.
5 After the concert, I **struck up** a conversation with the guitarist.

36.6
1 Ben's not keen on buying a new car. I'm trying to **talk** him **round.**
2 When soccer **came up in** conversation, Bill and I realized we support the same team.
3 Craig was trying to tell a joke, but **tailed off** as he realized that no one was listening.
4 While Julia was explaining her idea, Rupert **cut in** to tell her she was wrong.
5 Simone spent the whole of lunch **mouthing off** about how much she hates her new boss.

37

37.3
1 tomar apuntes
2 reducir en tamaño
3 redactar algo a partir de apuntes
4 escribir algo rápido o en borrador
5 ser la abreviatura de
6 leer con mucha atención
7 rellenar un formulario

37.4
1 Before you can use the gym, you need to fill in this form.
2 As the judge read out the names of the winners, Pablo waited hopefully.
3 When completing the form, Damian wrote in his age.
4 Alexandra flicked through a magazine while she waited to get her hair cut.

37.5
1 Max **read through** the full report before giving his opinion.
2 Ted always **writes out** his essays instead of typing them.
3 "UFO" **stands for** Unidentified Flying Object.
4 The journalist **jotted down** the details as Dan described his role in the new movie.
5 Fatima **read up** on ancient Greece before her history exam.

37.6
1 I'll try to cut **out** 500 words from my essay if it is too long.
2 *Adventures in the Wilderness* should make **for** interesting reading!
3 Paco read the book and noted **down** the most important points.
4 We **pored over** the old document looking for clues.

38

38.4
1 Rob wants to **follow** up on the conversation we had about the new logo.
2 Claudia sent wedding invitations **out** to all her friends and family.
3 Dave passed **on** a message telling me that Rob had called.
4 Sorry, I can't hear you very well, I'm afraid. You keep **breaking** up.
5 I've called Olly a few times this evening, but I can't get **through.**
6 Could you please speak **up**? I can't hear you very well!

38.5
1 Chris emailed me a week ago, but I only just remembered to email him back.
2 Murat completed all the forms and sent them off to the passport office.
3 I love receiving letters from my dad. I always write back immediately.
4 Claudia sent wedding invitations out to all her friends and family.

38.6
1 put through 2 pick up 3 call back
4 speak up

38.7
1 Anna works from home on Tuesdays, so she will **dial into the** meeting.
2 I'll **put you through** to Mr. Yamamoto now, madam.
3 Our company is trying to **reach out to** new customers by offering discounts.
4 After chatting for over an hour, Simon and I said goodbye **and hung up.**
5 Hi Laura, sorry I'm cooking at the moment, can I **call you back** in 10 minutes?

39

39.4
A 3 B 1 C 7 D 2 E 5 F 4 G 8 H 6

39.5
1 When my husband suggested buying a new kitchen, I did what he suggested.
2 When I told my friends I was starting my own business, they all offered support.
3 They gave us too much information during the training course.

4 Experts believe that Joan Miró created this painting because of the distinctive style.
5 The artist's feelings of anger are communicated strongly in this painting.

39.6

SEPARABLES:
bombard with
bounce off
think over
think through
put to

INSEPARABLES:
run with
come across
touch on
come up with
get behind

39.7

1 The creative manager asked her team to **throw out** as many ideas as they could.
2 It finally **dawned on** me that Claude was the killer.
3 We have **ruled out** three of the candidates. It's a choice between Danny and Carmen.
4 Ted has **come up** with some good ideas for a new logo.
5 Selma is very creative. She **thinks up** lots of wonderful dishes.

40

40.2

1 expand on
2 dumb down
3 come back to
4 point out
5 go back over

40.3

1 put across **2** dumb down
3 point out **4** come back to
5 allude to **6** go back over

41

41.3

1 see through
2 gloss over
3 cover up

4 add up
5 fall for
6 make up
7 level with

41.4

1 make out
2 level with
3 mess around
4 add up
5 put on
6 catch on

41.5

1 I think she knows more than she's **letting on**.
2 We **fell for** the salesman's talk. The car we bought broke down after a few days.
3 When it **came out** that he was bankrupt, I was shocked!
4 Conan finally **owned up** to breaking the window. He'd been denying it all morning.
5 The CEO has been **playing down** the company's financial problems.
6 I've been trying to **find out** from Nisha who Sammy's dating.
7 Josie tried to **explain away** the damage to my car by saying it was just a small scratch.

42

42.2

1 Helen has put me onto this great new hair salon. I'm going to check it out.
2 Lisa's speech in favor of a new nature reserve has brought many people around to the idea.
3 Kendra was very nervous, but was happy to see her friends rooting for her.
4 Zoe's daughter said her elder brother had put her up to stealing the cookies.

42.3

1 Kendra was very nervous, but was happy to see her friends **rooting for** her.
2 Rahul was skeptical about electric cars until the salesman **reasoned with** him.
3 The crowd **urged** Mona **on** as she approached the end of the tightrope.
4 He eventually **won** him **over** by explaining how eco-friendly they are.
5 My son was upset, so I bought him an ice cream to **buck** him **up**.

43

43.3

1 During the debate, she hit out at her opponents.
2 I can count on my sister to comfort me when I'm upset.
3 Paul usually shrugs off criticism of his cooking.
4 Carla stood up to the bullies and told them not to be mean.
5 He pulled her up on her attitude towards the environment.

43.4

B, **C**, **D**, **F**, **H**, **I**

43.5

1 Everyone agrees **with** John that Sian should get the job.
2 Everyone criticized Magda's art, but she rose **above** it and is a successful artist now.
3 The workers are pushing **back on** the management's policies.
4 They disagreed **with** each other about what color to paint the kitchen.

43.6

1 Mi tía lo desaprueba.
2 Paulina siempre apoya a nuestro jefe.
3 Laura se ha opuesto a las propuestas.
4 Carla se defendió.
5 Deben solucionar pequeños problemas..

43.7

1 I think Sonia **has** something **against** me. She never wants to talk to me.
2 Martin and Simon **disagreed with** each other about what color to paint the kitchen.
3 Our local representative has **come out against** the plans for a new housing development.
4 Donna bought her brother some chocolates to **make up for** the things she had said to him.
5 Terry's colleagues always make fun of his shirts, but he just **laughs** it **off**.

44

44.4

1 back off **2** speak out **3** take back
4 stay out of **5** patch up **6** base on
7 stick up for

44.5

Ⓐ 3　Ⓑ 6　Ⓒ 1　Ⓓ 2　Ⓔ 5　Ⓕ 4

44.6

1 back off　2 stay out of
3 back up　4 stick up for
5 fall out (with)　6 lash out (at)
7 back down

44.7

1 When Pete showed Martin the facts, Martin had to **climb down** and admit he was wrong.

2 The manager **laid into** the players after they lost another match.

3 They had **fallen out** when they both applied for the same job.

4 Craig's parents finally caved **in** and bought him a games console.

5 Sorry, I'm not sure what you're **getting at**.

45

45.3

1 Ed está más fuerte.

2 Me ha ayudado a gestionar mis problemas.

3 Kathy está intentando recuperarse.

4 Anna cada vez es más feliz.

45.4

1 work through
2 crack up
3 settle down
4 light up
5 burst out

45.5

1 Donny's face lit **up** when he saw the presents waiting for him on the table.

2 Jack's a very private person, but he finally opened **up** and told me how he feels.

3 When Linda feels stressed, she listens to music to help her calm **down**.

4 The children burst **out** laughing when the clown pretended to fall over.

45.6

1 I've been **checking up on** Andrei every day since he lost his job.

2 Craig had had a bad day at work, but watching a funny movie **cheered him up**.

3 Hiro's jokes are hilarious. He really **cracks me up**.

4 Yana was upset, but she **brightened up when** I bought her tickets to a concert.

45.7

1 Sophie needs to **lighten up**. She's still studying even though it's her birthday today.

2 I really **feel for** Kim. She's been so upset since her cat went missing.

3 Kathy is finally **moving on** after her breakup with Jamal last year.

4 Petra's been sulking for days. I wish she'd **snap out of** it.

46

46.2

1 My husband tenses up whenever **I try to talk about money with him**.

2 This song is so moving. **It always sets me off**.

3 Troy freaked out when he noticed **the enormous spider climbing up the wall**.

4 Clare flew into a rage when **her computer crashed and lost all her work**.

5 Stop taking it out on me. **It's not my fault the weather is awful**.

6 My grandchildren love to wind me up. **They're always playing tricks on me**.

46.3

1 Sadie's anger about her boss's rude behavior had been **building up**.

2 Tamal and Sam **choked up** when the hero died at the end of the movie.

3 When Lisa walked onto the stage she **froze up**. She couldn't say anything!

4 He eventually **broke down** and admitted that he was really upset.

5 My manager **blew up** when I told him that I'd left my work laptop on the train.

46.4

1 Bella **welled up** when Pete asked her to marry him.

2 It eventually **spilled over**, and Sadie told her how she felt.

3 Chris had been **bottling up** his emotions for a long time.

4 Work has been **weighing on** me a lot recently.

5 Clare **flew into** a rage when her computer crashed and lost all her work.

46.5

1 get down
2 wind up
3 break down
4 blow up

47

47.2

1 Sonia opted **out** of the boat trip. She always gets sea sick.

2 Yasmin has been toying **with** the idea of getting her hair cut short.

3 The workers wanted a 5% pay raise, but settled **for** 3%.

4 Shona regrets her decision to quit, but she's going to have to live **with** it.

5 After a lot of thought, Rob went **for** the fish instead of the steak.

47.3

1 decide on
2 factor in
3 mull over
4 pick out
5 opt out
6 lean toward

47.4

1 weigh up　2 narrow down　3 pick out
4 sleep on　5 lean toward

47.5

1 Moving to New Zealand next year **hinges on us** saving enough money.

2 Can you tell us how you **settled on a** winner?

3 Lisa found it hard to choose a dress, but eventually **decided on the** red one.

4 Stephen is **banking on this** new recipe to impress his guests.

48

48.2

Ⓐ 3　Ⓑ 5　Ⓒ 1　Ⓓ 4　Ⓔ 2

48.3

1 I was relying on Selma to bring candles for the cake, but she **let** me **down**.

2 I'll never **live down** the time I dropped Erin's birthday cake in the middle of her party.

3 Coralie's graph didn't make sense, so she looked through the data again to see where she'd **slipped up**.

4 When Chris got home from work, he realized that he had **mixed** his bag **up with** Simon's.

5 The spelling mistake in Juanita's homework **jumped out at** me.

49.4
❶ After the leak in the room above, it looked like the ceiling might fall in.
❷ The dog knocked over the plant pot as it chased the cat.
❸ Jorge took the old clock apart to fix it.
❹ When I got home, I found that the dog had torn a cushion apart.

49.5
Ⓐ 3 Ⓑ 1 Ⓒ 4 Ⓓ 6 Ⓔ 2 Ⓕ 5

49.6
❶ smash up
❷ wear out
❸ bang into
❹ trip over
❺ fall in
❻ break off

49.7
❶ I **banged into** the door while leaving the house.
❷ Colin accidentally drove into a tree and **smashed up** his van.
❸ Rodrigo slammed the door so hard that the pictures **fell off** the wall.
❹ The old book **came apart** in the librarian's hands.
❺ The drain was **clogged up** with old leaves, so I had to unblock it.
❻ Sanjay's old car is **falling apart**. He's had it since he was a teenager.
❼ The old manor house Andrei wants to buy looks as if it's about to **fall down**.

50

50.2
Ⓐ 5 Ⓑ 1 Ⓒ 6 Ⓓ 4 Ⓔ 2 Ⓕ 3 Ⓖ 8 Ⓗ 7

50.3
❶ Whenever Gitanjali has a problem, she goes to her grandmother for advice.
❷ While climbing the mountain, we had to deal with strong winds and heavy rain.
❸ The proposals for a new highway have encountered a lot of local opposition.
❹ One of the pipes was leaking, so we asked a plumber to fix it.
❺ Writing your thesis is easier if you separate it into small sections.

❻ It's taken me all evening to find out how to turn on this new television.

50.4
SEPARABLES:
break down
thrash out
brush aside
think through

INSEPARABLES:
turn to
come up against
crop up
get around

50.5
❶ turn out ❷ think through ❸ sort out
❹ clear up ❺ brush aside ❻ thrash out
❼ check out

51

51.3
❶ I didn't mean to tell the team **that it was your birthday. It just slipped out.**
❷ The movie star tried to hush up **the fact that she had a new boyfriend.**
❸ Jessica has been keeping **the name of her new boyfriend from me.**
❹ I was bowled over when Nadia announced **that she had been accepted into dance school.**
❺ Mollie crept up on her grandfather **while he slept in the garden.**

51.4
❶ Clara can't believe she passed her exams. It's going to take a while for it to sink **in**.
❷ People have woken **up** to the fact that we need to look after the environment.
❸ I was shopping at the antiques market when I stumbled **upon** a valuable necklace.
❹ My best friend **sprang** it on me last night that she's moving to Canada.
❺ I was taken **aback** when Tia and Juan told me they were getting married.

51.5
❶ play along ❷ bump into ❸ cotton onto
❹ give away

51.6
❶ I stumbled upon a valuable necklace at the antiques market.
❷ Jessica has been keeping the name of her new boyfriend from me.

❸ Mollie crept up on her grandfather while he slept in the garden.
❹ We were all eating our dinner when the dog burst into the room.

52

52.4
❶ sacar
❷ aparecer (en la pantalla)
❸ hacer algo para solucionar un problema
❹ tener opinión sobre algo
❺ ir hacia un lugar
❻ huir con algo
❼ eliminar, no hacer falta

52.5
Ⓐ 6 Ⓑ 5 Ⓒ 1 Ⓓ 3 Ⓔ 2 Ⓕ 4

52.6
❶ Riya was disappointed with her wedding cake, and insisted it be **done over**.
❷ With hot weather expected, thousands of tourists **made for** the coast.
❸ Lots of talented people **make up** our circus's team of acrobats.
❹ Natsuo **came across** the room to speak to us.
❺ The council has to decide what it's going to **do about** the litter problem.
❻ Luanne struggled to **make out** what the train conductor was saying.
❼ No matter how much we clean it, this graffiti won't **come off** the wall.

52.7
❶ Hetty's career as a musician **came about** after a producer saw her performing.
❷ Derek sat down in front of the TV when the ten o'clock news **came on**.
❸ Luanne struggled to **make out** what the train conductor was saying.
❹ When I tried to log in, a message **came up** saying that my account had been blocked.
❺ Lots of talented people **make up** our circus's team of acrobats.

53

53.3
❶ Cheryl's dog keeps **getting over** the fence into the neighbor's backyard.
❷ Harry burned the dinner and **set off** the smoke detector.

3 As Martin walked home late at night, fear began to **set in**.

4 It's almost eleven o'clock. We should **get down to** work.

5 Mary **set out** all her qualifications and experience in her resume.

6 Lee's speed **sets him apart from** the other players in the tournament.

53.4

SEPARABLES:

set back
set on
get across
get together

INSEPARABLES:

get around
get up (from)
get to
set in

53.5

1 set on   **2** get to   **3** set back
4 get back at   **5** get across
6 get together   **7** set up

53.6

1 Lee **got** his fishing **rod out** of the garage and carried it to his car

2 The security guard threatened to **set** his dog **on** us if we didn't leave immediately

3 Can you help me **get** the shopping **in**, please?

4 Before accusing Simon, the police had to **get** their facts **together**.

5 As soon as we **got to** the ski resort, we went straight to the slopes.

54

54.2

1   My daughter attends ballet classes every Saturday morning.

2   There's something happening next door. I can hear loud music.

3   James reviewed the company's accounts to check for mistakes.

4   Help yourself to some cakes. There are enough for everyone.

5   Malachai experienced a period of unhappiness after his dog died.

6   After I got back from the dentist, it took a couple of hours for the pain to disappear.

54.3

A 5   **B** 1   **C** 2   **D** 6   **E** 4   **F** 3
G 8   **H** 7

54.4

1 Michelle and I go back years. I've known her since kindergarten.

2 My new trainer is called Zachariah, though he usually goes by Zac.

3 Buying water in plastic bottles goes against my principles.

4 As soon as I realized Orla had forgotten her bag, I went after her.

5 The children watched the hot-air balloon slowly go up into the air.

54.5

1 Parents often have to **go** without sleep when they have a new baby.

2 Help yourself to some cakes. There are enough to go **around**.

3 Kelly's decided to go **for** the job at the software company. It's very well paid.

4 Rob and I sat on the beach watching the sun **go** down.

5 A team of firefighters went **into** the burning building.

6 All the money we make today will go **toward** funding the new school library.

7 Even though it was a cloudy day, Ramon decided to go **ahead** with the picnic.

55

55.4

1 Cassie followed the instructions carefully to put her new wardrobe together.

2 The waste collectors came to take away the bags of trash.

3 Martha played the violin as a child, but gave it up when she left school.

4 The police stopped the criminal, and took the stolen money from him.

5 Liam finished decorating the cake and put it on a stand.

55.5

1 The café on the high street is **giving** out samples of their new range of cookies.

2 Denise took a jar **down** from the shelf to give her dog a biscuit.

3 Angela is upset about her divorce, but she's trying to **put** it behind her.

4 Seeing the black clouds, Tim went outside to take the washing **in**.

5 My son had been asking for an ice cream all day. I finally **gave** in and bought him one.

55.6

1 The fitness instructor put the class **through a tough training program**.

2 Scarlett had to put up with **busy trains every day on her way to work**.

3 Angela is upset about her divorce, **but she's trying to put it behind her**.

4 Amara took her mother aside **to tell her that she was pregnant**.

5 The café on the high street is giving **out free samples of their new cakes**.

6 Eliza has really taken to golf. **She never thought she'd like it**.

7 Jim's mother asked him to take **his younger brother along to the skate park**.

55.7

1 Denise took a jar down from the shelf to give her dog a biscuit.

2 Angela is upset about her divorce, but she's trying to put it behind her.

3 Seeing the black clouds, Tim went outside to take the washing in.

4 Eliza has really taken to golf. She never thought she'd like it.

5 Amara took her mother aside to tell her that she was pregnant.

56

56.2

1 fire away   **2** come in   **3** bring it on
4 go ahead

56.3

1 go away   **2** look out   **3** go ahead
4 fire away   **5** bring it on   **6** get out
7 come on   **8** come in

Índice de phrasal verbs

Los números remiten al
número del módulo.

go back to **23.1**
go by **15.1**, **54.1**
   ver también bygone **R6**
go down **12.1**, **32.1**, **54.1**
go for **47.1**, **54.1**
go forward **16.3**
go in(to) **54.1**
go into **23.1**
go off **3.1**, **8.1**, **27.3**, **30.1**, **35.1**
go on **54.1**
   ver también ongoing **R6**
go out **3.2**, **5.1**, **27.3**, **54.1**
   ver también outgoing **R6**
go over **54.1**
go through **19.1**, **54.1**
go through with **17.1**
go to **54.1**
go together **30.1**
go toward **54.1**
go under **24.1**
go up **54.1**
go with **6.1**
go without **54.1**
goof off (US) **21.2**
grow into **6.1**
grow out of **2.1**, **6.1**
grow up **2.1**

H

hack into **12.1**
hammer out **17.1**
hand in (to) **21.1**
hand out (to) **21.1**
hand over **13.1**
hang on **15.2**
hang out **5.1**, **28.1**
hang over **50.1**
hang up **6.1**, **38.1**
have (something) against **43.1**
have off **22.3**
have over **4.1**
head for **35.1**
head off (to) **5.2**, **8.1**
head up **23.1**
heal up (UK) **32.1**
hear about **18.1**
hear from **3.1**

hear out **18.1**
heat up **29.1**
hinge on **47.1**
hire out (UK) **5.1**
hit out at **43.1**
hold up **15.2**
hurry up **15.1**
hush up **51.1**

I

impact on **7.1**
improve on **7.2**
incoming **R6**
input **R5**
intake **R5**
invite along (to) **4 .1**
invite in **4.1**
invite over **4.2**
iron out **43.2**

J

join in **33.1**
jot down **37.1**
jump out (at) **48.1**

K

keep at **31.1**
keep from **33.1**, **51.1**
keep up (with) **20.1**, **33.1**
kick back **31.2**
kickoff **R5**
knock down **10.1**
knockdown **R6**
knock out (of) **33.1**
knock over **49.1**
knuckle down **22.3**

L

land in **48.1**
lash out (at) **44.1**
laugh off **43.2**
launch into **36.1**
lay into **44.1**
lay off **24.1**

lay out **20.2**
laze about **31.2**
lead to **7.1**
lead up to **16.1**
lean toward **47.1**
leave behind **48.1**
leave on **27.3**
leave out **29.2**
leftover **R6**
let down **48.1**
letdown **R5**
let in **2.2**
let off (with) **21.2**
let on **41.1**
let out **2.2**, **6.1**
let up **11.1**
level out **25.1**
level with **41.1**
lie ahead **16.1**
lie around **31.2**
lie down **8.2**
lift up **19.1**
   ver también uplifting **R6**
light up **45.1**
lighten up **45.1**
line up **10.1**
listen in (on) **18.1**
listen out for **18.1**
listen to **18.1**
listen up **18.1**
live down **48.1**
live for **31.1**
live off **14.1**
live on **14.1**
live up to **7.2**
live with **2.1**, **47.1**
liven up **5.1**
lock away **27.1**
lock in **27.1**
lock out **27.1**
log in(to) **12.1**
log out (of) **12.1**
look after **2.1**
look ahead **17.1**
look around **10.1**
look at **18.3**
look away **18.3**
look back (on) **16.2**

look down on **1.1**
look for **18.3**
look forward to **16.1**
look into **18.3**, **20.1**
look on **18.3**
look out **56.1**
look out for **18.3**
look out over **18.3**
look over **18.3**
look through **18.3**
look up **20.1**
look up to **1.1**
loosen up **31.2**
lose out (to) **26.2**

M

made-up **R6**
major in (US) **20.1**
make for **37.2**, **52.2**
make into **34.1**
make of **52.2**
make off with **52.2**
make out **41.2**, **52.2**
make up **41.2**, **44.3**, **52.2**
   ver también made-up **R6**
make up for **43.2**
mark down **20.2**
measure out **29.1**
measure up (to) **7.2**
meet up (with) **22.2**
mess around **21.2**, **41.2**
mess up **49.1**
mill around **5.1**
miss out **48.1**
mist over **46.1**
mix in **29.1**
mix up (with) **48.1**
mix-up **R5**
mock up **34.1**
mop up **28.1**
mount up **25.1**
mouth off **36.1**
move along **19.1**
move away **27.2**
move in(to) **27.2**
move on **20.2**, **45.2**
move out (of) **27.2**

Agradecimientos

El editor quiere agradecer a:

Ankita Awasthi Tröger y Hina Jain, por su asistencia editorial; Anna Scully y Noopur Dalal, por su asistencia en el diseño; Laura Caddell, por la corrección; Christine Stroyan, por la gestión de la grabación del audio; ID Audio, por la grabación y la producción del audio; Harish Aggarwal, por su trabajo de maquetación; Priyanka Sharma, por la coordinación editorial de las cubiertas; y Saloni Singh, por la gestión de la edición de las cubiertas.

Todas las imágenes son propiedad de DK. Para más información, por favor, visite **www.dkimages.com**